PEER PRODUCTION

The MIT Press Essential Knowledge Series

A complete list of books in this series can be found online at
https://mitpress.mit.edu/books/series/mit-press-essential-knowledge-series.

PEER PRODUCTION

BENJAMIN MAKO HILL,
CHRISTIAN PENTZOLD,
AND AARON SHAW

The MIT Press | Cambridge, Massachusetts | London, England

The MIT Press
Massachusetts Institute of Technology
77 Massachusetts Avenue
Cambridge, MA 02139
mitpress.mit.edu

The open access edition of this book was made possible by generous funding and support from MIT Libraries.

The MIT Press would like to thank the anonymous peer reviewers who provided comments on drafts of this book. The generous work of academic experts is essential for establishing the authority and quality of our publications. We acknowledge with gratitude the contributions of these otherwise uncredited readers.

This book was set in Chaparral Pro by New Best-set Typesetters Ltd. Printed and bound in the United States of America.

Library of Congress Cataloging-in-Publication Data is available.

ISBN: 978-0-262-05480-5

10 9 8 7 6 5 4 3 2 1

EU Authorised Representative: Easy Access System Europe, Mustamäe tee 50, 10621 Tallinn, Estonia | Email: gpsr.requests@easproject.com

CONTENTS

The MIT Press's publishing mission benefits from the generosity of our donors, including Robert Pozen.

SERIES FOREWORD

The MIT Press Essential Knowledge series offers accessible, concise, beautifully produced pocket-size books on topics of current interest. Written by leading thinkers, the books in this series deliver expert overviews of subjects that range from the cultural and the historical to the scientific and the technical.

In today's era of instant information gratification, we have ready access to opinions, rationalizations, and superficial descriptions. Much harder to come by is the foundational knowledge that informs a principled understanding of the world. Essential Knowledge books fill that need. Synthesizing specialized subject matter for nonspecialists and engaging critical topics through fundamentals, each of these compact volumes offers readers a point of access to complex ideas.

PREFACE

Some popular histories of the internet begin in the 1960s with the US military funding the Advanced Research Projects Agency Network (Arpanet), touch quickly on the invention of the web by Tim Berners-Lee in the early 1990s, and then jump to the dot-com boom and turn of the millennium to describe how large tech companies like Apple, Amazon, Google, and Meta ushered in the business and technical innovations that constitute the internet today. These stories emphasize a state- and market-driven path to technological innovation; justify the power, control, and wealth of the big institutional players that have shaped the contemporary information economy; and imply that a cyberlibertarian policy agenda will best support the internet's future development.

We have written this book to correct such stories and fill in a crucial missing part. In fact, many of the internet's most important achievements were created by groups of hobbyists and volunteers working together outside markets, states, or firms through peer production: a way of aggregating the contributions of largely unremunerated individuals into public goods. Peer production represents the internet's most important organizational innovation, and has led to some of its most dazzling social and technical achievements. Inconveniently (at least for those who would prefer the market- and state-centric story), peer production involves scant monetary incentives, prices, or rewards; little to no central planning or hierarchical organization; and hardly any charismatic CEOs or solitary geniuses. Instead, the story of peer production is about more or less regular people, working outside formal organizations to solve their own problems and share the results with others. It is the story of Wikipedia, free/libre and open source software (FLOSS), and many thousands of other projects, the vast majority of which you have never heard of.

Most important, the story of peer production is about how the internet and digital media as we know it came to be. It highlights the role that cooperative ways of organizing have played in the development of the internet. Not only is cooperative production outside markets possible online, but much of the digital landscape today would not exist without it. While many assume that government investment and unfettered venture capital are the only ways to create technological and information infrastructure, they are not even the only ways we have done so in the last thirty years.

Today, peer produced projects form infrastructure that we all rely on every single time we use the internet. They provide the technical resources that run our phones and servers, organizational models that support businesses, and software and data that drive search, artificial intelligence (AI), and more.

We first talked about the idea for this book in late summer 2017 at the Center for Advanced Study in the Behavioral Sciences at Stanford University. We came from different countries, backgrounds, and academic perspectives, but all agreed on the need for a general, accessible introduction to peer production. Nearly ten years later, we believe that this need has only grown. The most recent monograph to discuss peer production in a comprehensive way—*The Wealth of Networks* by Yochai Benkler—was published twenty years ago. The intervening decades have witnessed both the continued influence and success of peer production as well as escalating challenges and threats to its viability. Enormous changes have also emerged in the ways practices and concepts from peer production have been taken up and incorporated into other domains.

There was a time, really not so many years ago, when the potential of peer production alongside other sorts of mass online collaboration inspired grand utopian visions and enthusiasms. That time has largely passed. Today, public debate about digital technology is dominated by concerns over AI. Discussion of online participation and social media is dominated by the various harms, fears, and adverse effects associated with misinformation, polarization, incivility, social isolation, and smartphone-enabled depression and anxiety. The juxtaposition is striking and sobering.

In writing this book, we aim to reinvest some—but not all—of the utopian, egalitarian, and cooperative energy into public conversations about digital technology as well as the things people do with it. We strive to do so without falling into naive, nostalgic, or uncritical ways of thinking. Most of all, we aspire to tell a story of what peer production has been and what it might become. We hope this book provides a guide that is helpful in documenting what has occurred, summarizing what we've learned, and reflecting on what it all means for the near future.

1

INTRODUCTION: WHAT IS PEER PRODUCTION, AND WHY DOES IT MATTER?

In 1991, a Finnish graduate student in computer science named Linus Torvalds sent a short announcement to an online discussion group explaining that he had been working on parts of a new operating system in his spare time. Torvalds described his project as "just a hobby [that] won't be big and professional," and insisted that it would be free to use, study, modify, and distribute. He was building a technically challenging piece of software called an operating system kernel, which handles the most basic functions related to communication between a computer's hardware and software. Unlike operating system projects of the past, Torvalds invited feedback and contributions from anybody on the internet. With time, Torvalds's kernel attracted other developers, who then worked with him to turn the hobby project into an established piece of software that the group called "Linux." This team combined their new kernel with another internet-based collaborative project called GNU whose goal was to create a replacement for the UNIX operating system, but that had not yet tackled the project of building a kernel. The result was the GNU/Linux operating system.

Nearly thirty years later, GNU/Linux (or just Linux—as most people call it) runs on billions of computers worldwide and has become one of the most important pieces of software in history. Nearly all supercomputers, a large majority of internet servers, a majority of smartphones, and a growing number of "embedded systems" in devices like televisions run some version of Linux. In all of these markets, Linux did not simply fill an empty niche. For example, GNU/Linux completely outcompeted or replaced proprietary server operating systems, including Solaris by Sun Microsystems, HPUX by HP, AIX by IBM, and others.

The success of Linux upended the prevailing wisdom about how to build software. In the 1980s and 1990s, most world-class software was written by large, hierarchically managed teams of developers within immense, multinational corporations like IBM, AT&T, DEC, or Microsoft (itself an upstart of sorts at that time). Software developers worked full-time for these companies and were well paid to do so. The companies retained vast legal teams that used restrictive copyright licenses, proprietary patents, and technological measures to ensure that none of the code their developers wrote could ever be used—or in most cases, even *seen*—by anyone outside the firm.

Linux took nearly every aspect of this proprietary software development approach and threw it out the window. Over many years, the Linux kernel and GNU/Linux operating system were built by volunteers collaborating outside firms, without hierarchical management structures, the use of money as the primary incentive, and the typical legal or technical arrangements to restrict access, adaptation, or reuse of the underlying source code. The vast majority of Linux contributors only wrote small amounts of code. But despite this unusual model of production, Linux's high quality and growing market share were undeniable by the end of the 1990s. In response, firms whose business models did not depend on selling software began to redirect the effort and code produced by their developers to Linux. Over the years, as more and more development effort was invested by this mix of volunteers and paid professionals working in hundreds of different firms, Linux outperformed and outcompeted proprietary software written within some of the world's largest and richest firms.

Linux has inspired millions of attempts to build knowledge goods in a similarly open and collaborative manner. Although many of these were also software projects, the most famous is the free, collaboratively produced encyclopedia Wikipedia. Like Linux, Wikipedia started with an open call for volunteer contributions to "an encyclopedia that anyone can edit" in January 2001. As of fall 2025, Wikipedia includes about 65 million articles across more than 300 different language versions. In the English-language version alone, the articles were built through more than a billion distinct contributions or "edits" by more than 121 million different user accounts and many millions of anonymous contributors. Nearly all of these edits are from volunteers. Today, Wikipedia is one of the most visited websites in the world, and the largest and most comprehensive encyclopedia in history by nearly any metric.

The collaborative production that underlies Linux and Wikipedia has been used thousands of times at a smaller scale as well. For example, while preparing the syllabus for a class, a law professor named Andreas Fischer-Lescano stumbled across some dubious passages in the doctoral thesis of German politician and then minister of defense Karl-Theodor zu Guttenberg. Fischer-Lescano searched for them on the internet and discovered that they had been copied from other sources without credit. In February 2011, a Twitter user took up the issue and asked for help analyzing Guttenberg's dissertation thoroughly. Many volunteers joined GuttenPlag Wiki—a participatory online platform created for that purpose—and within a couple of days, the 270 or so pages of Guttenberg's thesis were marked up with detailed documentation of apparent plagiarism in many places. About a month later, Guttenberg resigned from all political offices based on the incriminating findings. The Federal Diet in Berlin felt obliged to discuss the matter, and the responsible university committee revoked Guttenberg's academic title based on the evidence collected by the GuttenPlag Wiki community. The media praised the contributors' joint effort, rapid results, and impact on the political agenda. The volunteers had swiftly coordinated with each other, bundled their contributions together, and made them freely available.

Although radically different in terms of size, scale, and scope, Linux, Wikipedia, and GuttenPlag Wiki are all examples of "commons-based peer production," a term coined in the early 2000s by a law professor named Yochai Benkler to describe these novel kinds of projects.[1] Of course, Linux, Wikipedia, and GuttenPlag Wiki are each instances of distributed production made possible by the internet. But so are sites like eBay and Instagram that work in substantively different ways. Benkler sought to identify the unique traits that made peer production so new and impactful, while differentiating it from other kinds of online collaboration and social media. Drawing on the work of Benkler and others, we propose the following definition of peer production:

> Peer production is a form of internet-based, distributed collaboration that shares four traits.

> First, peer production projects motivate participants to contribute using diverse incentives that are frequently nonmonetary. Second, peer production projects are decentralized in that they are collectively self-governed and organized by participants. Third, peer production projects are decentralized in terms of how tasks are executed. Fourth, the content created by peer production projects is protected as public commons.

Each of the four traits helps to distinguish peer production from prior forms of social and economic organization as well as other types of online platforms and communities. For example, peer production projects are similar to markets in that they rely on the distributed, self-directed actions of individuals to create information and other kinds of goods. Unlike markets, however, peer production involves neither financial incentives, prices, nor exclusive property regimes. Unlike firms or government organizations, peer production involves neither contractual obligations, predefined work plans, nor hierarchical forms of management and task assignment. While some people may contribute to peer production as part of their job, many do so as volunteers. When people do engage in peer production related to their jobs, employers usually do not dictate the type of peer production work that employees pursue.

The final trait—the fact that peer production creates resources protected as a commons (sometimes called a "common-property regime") distinguishes the outputs of peer production as public resources that anyone can access or use without money changing hands or the negotiation of cumbersome licensing agreements. This aspect of peer production was deeply important to Benkler, and helps justify the use of a specialized term to differentiate modes of production rooted in market-based exchange or government fiat from those that occur in peer production. Yet because the term "commons-based peer production" is a mouthful, we follow others—including Benkler himself—by shortening it to "peer production."

These characteristics defy conventional assumptions about organizations and economic production. According to classical economic wisdom, if you want people to collaborate and efficiently distribute the outputs of that collaboration, the best way to do so involves private for-profit firms that sell goods or services in an open market. Firms hire and pay employees who are then contractually bound to pursue the work assigned to them by managers. The products of the work these employees do become the property of the company, which puts a price on them, manages sales transactions, and distributes both salaries and any profits generated along the way. In theory, these techniques solve the challenges of aligning incentives, organizing tasks, and ensuring that the resulting outputs get distributed to the people willing as well as able to pay for them. The same body of wisdom suggests that when markets do not produce or distribute a particular good or service effectively, those resources will need to be provided by a government or public agency. For parts of the world, health care, education, and transportation infrastructure are illustrations of things typically left to the government. In these cases, the incentives, pricing, and distribution of the resources in question are all managed inside the bureaucratic machinery of the state, and paid for through public revenue collection like taxes.

Peer production represents an alternative to the behavioral models at the heart of classical economic wisdom. Neither contractual obligations, financial incentives, nor bureaucratic authority ensure that participants contribute their work, or that the work gets organized effectively. The resulting products are public commons protected as nonexclusive (rather than private) forms of intellectual property. This means that peer produced resources cannot fetch a direct price on the open market. Nor can access to peer produced resources be restricted and resold, as happens on privately owned internet platforms like Facebook or Google. Additionally, work in peer production is neither paid for nor managed through government funding, direction, or oversight. Uniquely, peer production projects retain collective, autonomous control over the scope of their work, legitimacy of their leaders' authority, and selection of tasks worth pursuing. In other words, peer production projects like Linux, Wikipedia, and GuttenPlag Wiki demonstrate models of knowledge production that follow different social and economic arrangements than those that have produced nearly all similar goods and services in the past.

Over time, the impact of peer production has grown. Although it often remains invisible, peer production supports critical economic and social activity. Like the example of Linux, peer produced knowledge goods have become universal digital infrastructure. People all over the world rely on peer production even when they are not actively contributing to or visiting the websites of peer production projects. Beyond Linux and Wikipedia, well-known examples of peer production include the Firefox web browser and online mapping project OpenStreetMap. Lesser-known instances include software like Apache and NGINX, which run the vast majority of web servers on the internet, and the ubiquitous encryption software package OpenSSL, which handles secure connections and authentication across billions of financial transactions and account sign-on activities.

Through these projects and others, peer production has become a normal part of our media-suffused lives. Almost any time you visit a website, enter a question into an AI chatbot or search engine, interact with a smartphone, make a financial transaction, or sign on to an online

Peer production projects retain collective, autonomous control over the scope of their work, legitimacy of their leaders' authority, and selection of tasks worth pursuing.

service, you rely on software that was created through voluntary and nonmarket means. Peer production has reshaped property regimes and enlarged the common stock of public knowledge. As such, it boosts the capacity of people to do more for and by themselves as well as cooperate with others. Key examples like Wikipedia or Linux affirm the efficacy and sustainability of this nonproprietary approach to supplying knowledge goods and services.

Peer production also opens pathways for other aspects of human flourishing. Cooperative institutions provide opportunities to work, share, and thrive in ways that advance important civic and moral virtues. Autonomous peer production communities have become, in the language of sociologist Eric Klinenberg, valuable forms of "social infrastructure" that benefit both individuals and collectives.[2] From this perspective, those involved in peer production retain and exercise the freedom to pursue autonomous goals by autonomous means as a way of preserving these freedoms for others too.

What are a bunch of unpaid volunteers doing at the heart of the modern commercial internet? How do these volunteers get anything done if nobody is in charge and nobody pays them for their work? Why should we trust anything these communities create to support so many fundamental parts of our digital lives? In this book, we introduce peer production and offer answers to these questions. Peer production projects confront and overcome complex challenges, sometimes more effectively or at a lower cost than available alternatives. At a time when many of the world's most powerful companies and governments struggle with misinformation, declining participation in civil society, and growing social divisions, peer production supplies examples from which we can learn.

Peer production has also inspired new kinds of organizing, innovation, and mass collaboration that do not strictly fit our definition but instead share traits, or conform in weak or ambiguous ways. For instance, many companies have abandoned or loosened hierarchies and adopted flexible contracts. Public sector projects have incorporated mass collaboration and coordination techniques first developed in peer production. Online sites such as Reddit, Yelp, GitHub, or Airbnb have built new models of information and resource sharing that draw from peer production while diverging in critical ways.

To take one, Reddit is a site where people join topically defined subcommunities (subreddits) in which they voluntarily share information in "posts," then vote and comment on those posts. The aggregation—also known as collaborative filtering—of the voting as well as commenting activity produces a collective sense of what's most interesting or important. This model was drawn from previous peer production projects including the Open Directory Project (discussed in chapter 3). Thinking back to our definition, we would say that Reddit relies on diverse,

At a time when the world struggles with misinformation, declining participation in civil society, and growing social divisions, peer production supplies examples from which we can learn.

nonmonetary motivations and decentralized goal setting and execution, but that the products have always been formally controlled by Reddit's corporate owners (i.e., not a commons). Reddit's owners initially adopted a permissive attitude toward data redistribution and reuse that made Reddit *function* like a commons. Over time, this changed as Reddit prepared for an initial public offering of stock. AI companies engaged in the bulk collection and reuse of Reddit data, raising the financial stakes and introducing threats to the site's viewership and engagement. In spring 2023, Reddit's owners restricted and started charging for access to their data, making the site much less like a commons and provoking a backlash among some of the most committed volunteer contributors. Legalistic distinctions about the ownership of the community-generated content and data turned out to have huge consequences.

Other examples illustrate different kinds of deviations from our definition. While Yelp is, similar to Reddit, a volunteer-powered site for filtering information that is not a commons, it further diverges from the peer production model by constraining activity in ways that make goal setting more centralized. Likewise, GitHub (which is now owned by Microsoft) supports the peer production of free/libre and open source software (FLOSS) that is distributed as commons, but certain data (like bugs and feature requests) are controlled privately. In cases like Airbnb, private companies generate profits from an activity (hosting guests through "couch surfing") that was previously managed in a nonmonetized way by peer production communities, such as Couchsurfing.com and Hospitality Club, which offered nearly identical services. The distinctions are not purely between commercial and noncommercial activity either. For instance, the Anti-Slavery Manuscripts project sought to transcribe about forty thousand handwritten documents from the abolitionist movement in the United States held by the Boston Public Library. To do so, its organizers engaged thousands of volunteers through a "citizen science" platform to digitize this important archive, all of which is now freely available and protected as a digital commons. The goal-setting and task distribution of this initiative remained completely under centralized control, though. In these ways, peer production provides a reference point for related ways of organizing work online. It is more important to understand the core traits of peer production as well as the mechanisms by which peer production works than to label any specific case as a "true" or "false" example.

So far, much of the conversation about peer production has happened among academic researchers like the three of us writing this book. The fact that peer production challenges traditional scholarly ideas about the advantages of markets and hierarchical management makes it an urgent topic for students of organization and knowledge management. Of course, peer production is hardly a scholastic affair. As our illustrations show, peer production has become a key arena of contemporary activity with enormous repercussions in the world. Despite the impact of some of its products, peer production as a model of organizing is still not widely discussed or understood. We have written this book in order to provide an accessible introduction to the topic and include more people in the conversation about its future.

Peer Production and Beyond

Today, there are millions of peer production projects. This includes FLOSS projects and apps to serve almost any technical need. It includes wikis inspired by Wikipedia that work in an array of genres to collect and organize knowledge on a wide variety of topics. It includes question-and-answer (Q&A) websites like Stack Overflow and maps such as OpenStreetMap. And it includes communities whose products—like collaborative filtering projects that aggregate opinions—are more diffuse than encyclopedia articles and software but no less impactful.

Despite all the fanfare about "the wisdom of crowds" and related phenomena, collaborative production on the internet remains both rare and challenging. For every case of a peer produced product, there are many unsuccessful attempts to build a collaborative community. Many of these failed efforts to build communities produce valuable knowledge commons themselves. For example, in a study of software commons, Charles Schweik and Robert English found that a large portion of successful software commons—nearly a majority—only involve a single developer writing code on their own and sharing it with the world.[3] These projects are entirely uncollaborative.

Since Benkler and others started writing about peer production, the nature of cooperation, work, and commercial activity online has shifted immensely. Some of the most fundamental peer production projects rejected capitalistic property regimes. The GNU/Linux distribution and Wikipedia have contributed to restructuring key industries of the knowledge economy, especially commercial reference publishing and software development. Over time, however, a complex interaction between commercial services and volunteer efforts has emerged. Major repositories of peer produced goods also have downstream impacts through AI and other systems that harness peer production's output. For instance, Google shows infoboxes full of facts drawn from peer produced knowledge bases alongside its search results, generative AI systems, and digital assistants like OpenAI's ChatGPT, and Apple's Siri answers questions using data from peer produced sources. As a result, peer production projects benefit people in indirect and invisible ways. Today, peer production sits alongside, and is intertwined with, for-profit models of knowledge sharing, venture-funded social media services, and numerous attempts to build hybrid commercial/peer production platforms.

As peer production communities have matured, they have encountered challenges and limitations too. These range from issues that peer production projects confront (and sometimes overcome) internally to concerns about the impact and implications of peer production in the world. The emphasis on freedom and nonmonetary incentives in many projects restricts participation to those who can afford not to be paid for their labor. As a consequence, peer production has proceeded most rapidly in the Global North, and tends to reflect the demographic attributes and interests of the wealthiest, most digitally literate, and most empowered subsets of the world's population. Inside communities, hierarchies and power relations have emerged, and sexism and harassment can be widespread. Additionally, projects that grow tend to become more formalized as they do so, resulting in open communities that are, at the same time, highly structured, bureaucratic organizations. New elites have formed within communities, developing new means of exercising power. Even when communities welcome newcomers, arriving volunteers frequently meet multiple obstacles that effectively exclude all but the most highly educated and internet-savvy individuals. Initiatives to overcome these and related challenges have met with mixed success.

Despite these challenges, peer production has continued to shape the world in both direct and indirect ways. As wikis, distributed software development, and related modes of online collaboration have become more widespread, they have influenced how more traditional organizations structure themselves. Also, a large group of internet-based entities have drawn inspiration from peer production while diverging from the definitional criteria we enumerated earlier in one or more ways. This includes the so-called sharing economy, crowdfunding, distributed computing, user-generated content production on commercial platforms like YouTube or Yelp, hacking and fabrication spaces in the DIY movement, social media systems, and even blockchain-based technologies like cryptocurrencies. In general, these models of organizing production are not peer production. That said, many of these efforts have drawn directly—and often explicitly—from peer production in the way they organize themselves. They are built using lessons and technologies gleaned from peer production.

By learning and drawing from peer production, these models of production use the internet and mass collaboration in new and surprising ways. Increasingly, both small start-ups and giant multinational corporations have adopted techniques developed in peer production to build private resources and advance private interests. Peer production remains the predecessor, and in many cases, explicit inspiration, for many collaborative models of online production. Understanding peer production is a crucial step in appreciating these and many other emergent forms of organization and production.

An Alternative Mode of Production

The rapid success of communities like the Linux kernel and Wikipedia shocked many observers who had not imagined that anything other than corporations, governments, or markets could create as well as sustain complex, high-quality knowledge goods. Peer production thus provides a surprising answer to a question asked in various ways for centuries: How can people work together to create and share public resources?

Historically, attempts to address this question have focused on the provision of things like sustainable natural resources, public infrastructure, and legitimate social institutions. Although these types of resources differ from peer production's archetypal products like software, encyclopedias, and maps in important ways, they offer a set of examples useful for understanding how and why peer produced goods have outcompeted private or public alternatives. Perhaps more intriguing, peer production supplies models for how people might use the internet to build public goods more effectively in the future.

While classical explanations of public goods production emphasize financial incentives such as exclusive property rights, there are other important nonmarket traditions. The most well-known are common-pool resource (CPR) regimes like Indigenous systems of water management in Bali and cooperative governance among lobster gangs in New England. Some of these systems existed for centuries before the rise of financial markets, nation-states, or other types of modern social organization (never mind the internet!). Some have proven far more reliable and effective at sustaining public goods than market or government-based alternatives.

In her Nobel prizewinning work, political economist Elinor Ostrom concluded that effective CPR management of fisheries, watersheds, and forests relies on autonomous self-governance to regulate the allocation of shared resources through the work of individuals drawn from among those impacted most directly by the regime.[4] Ostrom's insights into the governance of CPRs suggest alternative means by which societies can create, manage, sustain, and share important goods. Her work also shows how these arrangements complement governance models that rely primarily on markets, firms, or states. Peer production projects offer a setting in which to glean analogous insights into the management of knowledge commons. By autonomous, collaborative, and voluntary means, peer production projects create, share, and sustain valuable knowledge goods, such as software, encyclopedias, and maps. In this sense, peer produced digital infrastructure can be seen as the water, forests, and fisheries of the information age. Like more traditional public resources, the knowledge commons at the core of peer production also require maintenance and oversight to sustain their value. Many of the challenges as well as strategies to overcome them map from Ostrom's ideas about CPRs to peer production.

Nevertheless, while peer production shares much with historic examples of autonomous CPR management, it is different in critical respects too. Most of the documented instances of CPR governance dealt with tangible resources that were plentiful but ultimately finite (like forests or fisheries). Peer production sustains digital knowledge goods. These intangible resources, once created, are what economists describe as "nonrival" or "nonsubtractable" in that they can be copied and used an infinite number of times without any additional cost or reduction in the original. Consider that creating a copy of a digital music file does nothing to reduce the quality of the original. This is distinct from a fishery, where every fish caught means one less fish for everybody else. This unique feature of knowledge goods is at the center of peer production, and has allowed the value and scale of peer produced resources to grow far beyond what would have been possible with a traditional CPR. Unlike a forest, which contains a finite number of trees available for lumber or other uses, a Wikipedia article can be produced, copied, and read by everybody at effectively the same cost that it can be produced and read by a single person.

Although the tools used to sustain peer produced goods include strategies of self-management and collaborative governance similar to tangible CPRs, they typically have an added layer of legal instruments in the form of alternative copyright licenses. These licenses ensure that future products remain available for public access, use, and improvement. Peer production projects also employ novel features of governance made possible by digital infrastructure and software interfaces that earlier CPR systems did or could not use. These involve features like user accounts, automated rule enforcement, and distributed means of storage or access. To what extent is the success and growth of peer production due to these differences? Can they be adapted and applied outside peer production? What might traditional forms of public goods learn from successful peer production projects? The book explores these questions by placing peer production into a broader intellectual and historical context.

Moreover, we seek to explain why and how peer production works. As we have said, peer production violates many commonsense ideas about how large-scale cooperation, organization, or exchange occur. There is, however, no recipe for success. Most attempts to start new peer production communities never attract more than one or two contributors. Finding and sustaining success in peer production poses a distinct set of challenges.

We offer three explanations for how, why, and when effective peer production occurs. The first stresses the role of technology and social conditions. As a principle, specific tools and contexts make some activities harder or easier than others. This predates peer production. For example, movable type and printing presses needed to exist before there could be large-scale newspaper and publishing industries. Similarly, the technologies and historical conditions that gave rise to the internet helped make peer production possible. Digitally networked communications systems allowed people to interact across cultural, temporal, and spatial boundaries at a radically different scale than had ever happened before. In addition, the technical infrastructures and devices of the digital age allowed large, complex tasks to be broken into small, modular pieces that could then be distributed more quickly across many people. Broadband networks, collaboration software, and low-cost digital storage made it easier for those with the necessary skills as well as means to cocreate and use shared knowledge resources. These systems also made it easier for people to locate and contribute to projects and tasks that suited their passions and abilities. In sum, peer production is a product of the internet along with the way it has driven down the costs of connection, communication, and cooperation.

A second explanation focuses on the social processes that occur inside peer production projects. Although the existence of the internet and widespread access to computing devices makes distributed collaboration possible, it still requires an enormous amount of hard work to organize an effective peer production project. Leaders and participants in projects have to solve complex challenges if they are to recruit new participants, establish project goals, coordinate contributions, and manage the routines, norms, and rules necessary to sustain collaboration over the long haul. Participants have to develop a collaborative culture that supports sharing, trust, reciprocity, and other fundamental practices. Ideals of autonomy, cooperation, and self-governance can run up against hard, practical problems. Every successful peer production community we know of has experienced interpersonal conflict, abuses of authority, and threats from disgruntled or malicious participants. Individuals as well as whole communities must navigate these challenges.

The vast majority of peer production communities never overcome these organizational challenges to the point of building a critical mass of participants and getting their efforts off the ground. Even among successful communities, contributors come and go. Over time, a lot of projects decline in activity. Many reach an end of some sort within several years of launching. Explaining how and why some projects grow larger, and turn out more or less effective than other similar communities, requires us to dive into the details of everyday peer production at a deeper level.

The third explanation zooms in further to consider the motivations and actions of individual participants who freely share their time and knowledge with others. Why do they do it? What keeps these people coming back and working so hard when they do not get paid, or in some cases, even acknowledged? As the earliest projects like GNU and Linux emerged in the 1980s and 1990s, questions about the motivations of individual contributors drove the first academic studies of peer production. Surveys of these communities suggested that in the absence of direct financial compensation, peer production contributors were driven by a mix of collective and private incentives that resist a simple summary. Some participants seek extrinsic rewards like reputation gains and esteem among their peers, promotions to community leadership positions, or the acquisition of job-related skills and career benefits. Many participate in search of intrinsic gratifications such as fun, the experience of self-fulfillment and personal enhancement, or the satisfaction of engaging in a generous, public-spirited enterprise. These reasons have patterns that are important to understand in order to learn how communities and individuals uphold complex collaboration in the long run.

The Plan of This Book

This book advances three core ideas. First, peer production has become a critical mode of collaborative knowledge production that impacts billions of people on a daily basis. Second, peer production represents a novel type of social collaboration that extends our understanding of how people interact, organize, and advance collective interests. Third, peer production has unique advantages over previous forms of collaboration while suffering from a series of important challenges, some of which are distinct from those found in other enterprises. We have introduced these arguments above and will return to them.

Chapter 2 presents a brief history of peer production. We show how peer production emerged in the past thirty years or so from the context of FLOSS movements. Many of the most important achievements of peer production were facilitated by the "copyleft" principle created with the GNU General Public License (GPL). This ordering of intellectual property gives users the right to modify and distribute (modified) copies of peer produced works. In its original form, copyleft ensures that the same conditions apply to all derivatives of peer produced works. We also address the origin of the term "peer production" itself along with some early academic research on the subject to explain why peer production was so puzzling and unexpected when it first emerged.

Chapter 3 charts peer production's impact, and contends that peer production has shaped the internet and the world. We present some of the ways that peer production makes up much of the digital infrastructure that runs the modern world. This includes both technical infrastructure that supports the web and knowledge infrastructure that provides us with facts about the world as well as a sense of what is relevant or important. We also show how peer production has had profound indirect impacts by inspiring new organizational practices and forms.

Chapter 4 elaborates on the three explanations (introduced in the preceding section) for how effective peer production happens: first, an infrastructure-level explanation that emphasizes the importance of technologies and large-scale social forces; second, an organizational-level explanation focused on norms, governance, and collective intelligence; and finally, an individual-level explanation about participants' motivations and behavior. Although these explanations blend together, distinguishing between them helps illustrate how no single factor can capture the whole of peer production.

The challenges and limitations characteristic of peer production are the focus of chapter 5. Peer production projects routinely fall short in systematic ways analogous to the many types of market failures that characterize economic life. We discuss several of these challenges including failures in early stage project growth, entrenchment and abuses of power by community leaders, social conflicts and incivility, participant diversity and inclusion, and biased content production.

We end in chapter 6 by reflecting on the past, present, and future prospects for peer production. We suggest that the zenith of peer production as we have known it may have already passed, and the future seems likely to include the evolution and transmutation of peer production in new directions.

Throughout this book, we describe peer production with frequent references to key examples. Although readers will know the cases we lean on most heavily, like Wikipedia and Linux, others will be less familiar. We hope that these instances both illustrate salient concepts and demonstrate how peer production is a broader phenomenon than the handful of famous projects that have become household names. We note that our examples reflect geographic, linguistic, and cultural biases too; the majority originate or predominate in regions of the Global North, and involve languages and cultural groups familiar to the three of us. Although some of this bias derives from the inequities and gaps in online participation and peer production itself, some derive from our personal limitations and gaps of awareness as well. We have made efforts to address these latter types of constraints, but do not pretend to have succeeded completely. We take responsibility for the absences and omissions that may result, and encourage others to help us correct them in the future.

Along the way, we draw on the best available evidence to separate hype from reality. As scholars of peer production, we use empirical academic research to provide the foundation for many of our claims. Drawing on research also helps us introduce you to some of the most important concepts, findings, and thinkers that have shaped the practice and study of peer production in fields such as communication, computer science, management, cultural studies, law, and economics. We do our best to avoid unnecessary jargon, technical language, and arcane details better suited for academic publications. Where appropriate, we offer pointers to resources that interested readers may want to pursue to learn more, including a brief list of recommended readings at the end of this volume.

We wrote this book because we believe peer production is a crucial phenomenon that many people can benefit from learning about. We focus on basic principles, fundamental insights, and deep challenges from peer production in order to ensure that what follows speaks beyond the ephemeral specifics of any particular website or technology. Like nearly everything related to the internet and computing, peer production has evolved quickly in the last few decades and will continue to do so. Some aspects of this book and especially some of the examples may age quickly as a result. Yet the core arguments and ideas should, we hope, prove more durable. When the first piece of free software was released, not even its authors foresaw the emergence of peer production nor could they have imagined that anyone would still be writing about their work decades later. This is the story of how peer production surpassed all early expectations, why it has accomplished so much since, and where it might go next.

2

HISTORY AND CONTEXT: WHERE DID PEER PRODUCTION COME FROM?

Peer production started with a broken printer. In 1980, Richard Stallman, a twenty-seven-year-old staff software programmer at MIT's Artificial Intelligence Lab, sent a file to the lab's laser printer, which jammed due to a software problem. The machine, a donation from Xerox, was among the best available on the market, but was far from perfect. In the past, buggy computer hardware had never been a problem. After all, the lab was home to some of the world's most brilliant programmers who loved rolling up their sleeves to fix tricky technical issues. At the time, companies like Xerox had supported this kind of in-the-field troubleshooting by providing source code for drivers and other software. This allowed sophisticated users, like the folks at the AI lab, to inspect the code, find errors, create patches themselves, and get their printers back up and running. Valuable fixes would then be shared back to the company or made available to other users. Hardware vendors like Xerox profited from communities of engineers improving their tools.

But for Stallman that day, things were different. When he asked Xerox for drivers, he was told they would not be made available. The company executives had begun to view the ability to control software—and the exclusive rights to sell it—as a growing source of power and profit. Xerox was not the only firm pursuing this vision. Struggling with the printer and unable to access its code, Stallman realized that the norms of sharing and collaboration between technology companies and end users were eroding. The nondisclosure and commercialization of code repelled Stallman. So he set out to create a freely available alternative that preserved the spirit and practice of handing on as well as modifying software without restrictions or costs.[1]

Stallman's printer experience and his response turned out to be the first steps toward the creation of peer production as we know it today. In the history of free software, Stallman remains an important (and problematic) figure, who we will discuss in depth more.

Below, we trace how free software and peer production emerged alongside globally networked digital communication systems, the spread of near-ubiquitous personal computers, and the falling costs of processing capacity. We also show how the roots of peer production predate the internet, originating in the age of Enlightenment and the earliest days of the Industrial Revolution.

Cooperation and Collective Invention

At a basic level, cooperation involves individuals exchanging resources for collective benefit. Many anthropologists and biologists claim that cooperation explains key aspects of human evolution. At a minimum, cooperation is advantageous when a larger group is necessary to achieve something desirable that an individual person cannot. In this way, cooperation entails recognizing individual limits, interdependence, and the ability to indicate needs and negotiate relations.[2] It is not merely the absence of conflict. Interdependence fosters cooperation. Practicing cooperation lays the foundation for civility, the division of labor, and the formation of social life.[3]

Cooperative behavior underpins peer production and foundational virtues, such as trust, mutualism, equity, and fairness. Although the technical basis of peer production is a late twentieth-century phenomenon, its cooperative mode of providing goods and services has roots in many traditions and precursors. As a result, historical forerunners help contextualize commons-based interaction in ideologies around common property, the sharing of goods and labor, and democratic rule. All realize some traits we also associate with peer production.

One example is the *Encyclopédie*, a general compendium of human knowledge edited by Denis Diderot and Jean le Rond d'Alembert. Its publication started in 1751 and ended in 1772 with the last collection of illustrations. The finished *Encyclopédie* included a remarkable number of articles—71,818 in alphabetical order—and ran to 27 volumes. Scale alone does not distinguish the project, though. The most novel and ambitious aspect of Diderot and d'Alembert's plan was engaging the best and brightest thinkers of their time to write articles in parallel. To this end, the work was divided, and collaborators were invited to create those parts that fit their expertise.[4]

In the *avertissements* (forewords preceding the volumes), Diderot listed 143 "correspondents" in total. They came from different social ranks and professions. No women were mentioned, although historians believe female aristocrats likely penned some entries. Diderot himself authored the entry on "Encyclopédie," in which he explained the ideas guiding the project. The 35,000-word article began by stating that a single person or institution cannot write such a book. Only through collaboration could a federation of experts do so. The editorial challenge was to integrate and cross-reference the contributions from dozens of authors who differed in style, talent, and productivity. Given their diverse inputs and his limited capacity, Diderot was pragmatic enough to acknowledge that the first edition would suffer from all sorts of bias and disproportions. Still, the *Encyclopédie* reflected some of the most progressive political and philosophical thoughts on individual liberty, religious tolerance, and the power of reason at the time.

The relations among the correspondents of the *Encyclopédie* rested on reputation and esteem. A loosely connected, disparate group, the contributors approached knowledge as a higher-order good not subject to commercial exploitation or secrecy. As peers, they communicated via letters, or in clubs and salons, where they could deliberate and review each other's arguments. At its best, this republic of ideas fostered principles of communalism and universalism while rejecting the privileges that came with titles, income, or seniority. Members, also referred to as *philosophes* ("philosophers" in a general sense), judged each other based on the originality of their positions, separation of personal interests from intellectual opinions, and avowed skepticism toward all questionable claims.[5] These norms guided the rise of modern science and its methods. They undergird peer production too.

Another example is the *Oxford English Dictionary*, or *OED*. A vast undertaking, the *OED* took years and thousands of contributions to compile. A key moment came in April 1879 when the philologist and teacher James Murray issued a public appeal. The four-page pamphlet addressed all speakers and readers of English in Great Britain, the United States, and the British colonies of the time. In the document, Murray asked for help to complete a mission of titanic scope. A month earlier, he had been appointed editor in chief of a project to assemble all that was known of the English language. The resulting publication aimed to provide a comprehensive record of how English words were used and how their usage had changed. Work on this compendium had already begun in 1857, but it proved too vast to be completed on a tight schedule. Earlier dictionaries had been crafted by individual scholars who dedicated much of their lives to finding and cataloging words. In contrast, Murray's charge of compiling and annotating all English words would far exceed the capacity of even the most versatile genius. He needed help from anyone who would give it.

When the last volume of the first edition of the *OED* finally came out in 1928, the full collection included more than 1.8 million quotations from numerous sources. These examples encompassed past and present variants of English usage. Thousands of unpaid contributors worldwide had mailed in more than 5 million of these quotations on small slips of paper to Murray's so-called Scriptorium. The snippets were checked and sorted by a group of assistants. The original edition included 12 tombstone-sized volumes containing more than 15,000 single-spaced pages, cataloged 414,825 words, defined their meaning, recorded their provenance, and suggested pronunciations. A near 50-year undertaking, no single author could have erected such a monument in print.[6]

The *OED* aggregated contributions from diverse individuals. Some people contributed an enormous amount. Many contributed a single example. As such, the dictionary established a new mode of collaboration where a massive task was split into small ones and offered to the public to complete. Many people found the time and interest to cut out words from novels, plays, or newspapers, especially those they felt were peculiar, rare, or unusual. About one in six contributors appear to have been women. No one could know all the published English literature in the nineteenth and early twentieth centuries. But given the good-willed participation of many readers coupled with the immense and cumbersome work of the editors, the project was possible.

The ethos of knowledge exchange that pervaded the *Encyclopédie* and *OED* had other historical roots as well. In the early phases of industrialization, entrepreneurs, factory owners, and engineers shared technical knowledge freely and openly. For instance, in the United Kingdom during the late eighteenth and early nineteenth centuries, the iron industry of Cleveland and Yorkshire along with the mining industry in Cornwall thrived on competitors releasing details about the construction and height of blast furnaces and the performance of their pumping engines. Although they could have sought protection for particular design inventions of hot blast stoves under English patent law, they instead embraced a strategy that relied on making incremental improvements to the best available techniques and designs that came before.[7] These ad hoc collaborations, only possible because the patent system was not invoked, enabled collective invention, more efficient production, and wealth spillovers for all. Neither contracts nor brute force created this environment. Rather, inventors recognized the advantages of sharing in a common pool of knowledge and propagated the norms necessary to do so. Economic logic as opposed to altruistic principles led to sharing. The early industrialists all benefited far more from being able to build on others' work than by designing alone and trying to maintain exclusive rights.

These examples illustrate a long history of open, collaborative knowledge production, much of which emerged or grew alongside commercial markets and hierarchical organizations close to the origins of modern industrial capitalism. Peer production is a direct descendant of such initiatives and practices. In addition, however, peer production has incorporated distinct modes of collaborative organization and resource production, the roots of which lie elsewhere.

Markets, Firms, and the Commons

On October 12, 2009, Elinor Ostrom, a political science professor at Indiana University, got an early morning phone call from Stockholm, Sweden. Ostrom had just become the first woman to receive the Nobel Prize in Economic

Sciences. In its announcement, the Royal Swedish Academy of Sciences explained that Ostrom had "challenged the conventional wisdom by demonstrating how local property can be successfully managed by local commons without any regulation by central authorities or privatization." Over several decades, Ostrom studied the collective management of numerous commons, including mountain meadows in Switzerland, forests in Japan, and community irrigation systems in the Philippines and Spain. With these examples, Ostrom and her collaborators demonstrated that people could cooperate and organize for the sustainable provision and use of scarce resources. Ostrom's great contribution to the social sciences was to explain how such arrangements not only worked in practice but also in theory.[8]

Ostrom built on earlier work by economist Paul Samuelson, who defined public goods as nonexcludable (an inability to prevent other people from using a good) and nonrival (Ostrom often called it "nonsubtractability") to describe when the use of a good by someone did not prevent the use of the same item by someone else. Ostrom treated these two concepts as dimensions (excludability and rivalness) that depicted four possible types of goods.[9] Private goods are defined as being both excludable and rival commodities. So when one describes an apple as a private good, that implies it is rival. This means that if someone eats a particular apple, no one else will get a bite. Similarly, there are ways to exclude others to ensure no one else will savor your apple. The opposite is true for public goods. A classic public good might include useful knowledge, national security, or a sunset. For instance, you will likely have trouble excluding others from enjoying a sunset. Shared use is also rarely a problem for these goods because someone looking at the sunset need not interfere with you doing the same. Goods that are excludable but nonrival are called club goods. Examples include a private park or cinema. Although people can enjoy club goods without substantially impacting others' ability to do so, it is relatively easy to limit access. The fourth category is what Ostrom calls CPRs, like pastures or fisheries: highly rival yet largely nonexcludable goods. Although the word "commons" is frequently used interchangeably with CPRs (as it was in the Nobel Prize announcement), we follow others in using the term more generally to describe any shared resource in which stakeholders have a joint interest.

Managing CPRs is challenging because they cannot be easily protected from excessive use. With these resources, reasonable people (so-called rational actors) might maximize their benefit by taking as much of the resource as possible, such as grazing as many sheep as possible on public lands or cutting down all available trees. If others follow the same strategy, they will soon have ruined the resource, leaving everyone worse off. The tension between personal and social utility creates a contradiction: rational behavior at an individual level becomes irrational at a collective level. Ecologist Garrett Hardin called this "the tragedy of the commons" in an influential and controversial article by that name. According to Hardin, resource destruction is inescapable without some mechanism to support long-term and enduring usage.[10]

Traditionally, economists have advocated solving public goods and CPR challenges with state-enforced private property, prices, and markets. The earliest example of how this works comes from the "enclosure movement" that began in England around the thirteenth century. During that time, commonly held and managed pasturelands, forest groves, and lakes were physically fenced off and enclosed by members of the nobility, who then restricted access and use as they saw fit. Unsurprisingly, the process was often cruel, violent, and misery producing for those who could no longer draw on joint resources to graze sheep or cultivate crops. Many of these dispossessed peasant farmers were forced to relocate to cities and seek work in the nascent manufacturing industries.

The enclosure of CPRs made it possible to treat the land, trees, and water within as private property, and manage their access and exchange using market-based mechanisms. By putting prices on goods, markets can enable the efficient allocation of resources among large groups of people—but only under specific and frequently unrealistic conditions, with several important exceptions. In theory, markets allow for a low-cost form of coordination via prices that "solve" the tragedy of the commons. Yet the costs or challenges of allocating goods via markets can quickly become prohibitive. In these situations, firms—coordinated action by groups pursuing a shared goal—are often more effective than markets because they create islands of cooperation within competitive markets.

Instead of coordination and allocation through competition via prices, firms coordinate and allocate through employment contracts and bureaucracy. Another Nobel-winning economist, Ronald Coase, explained that firms would make and provide collective goods more efficiently than markets when uncertainty among trading parties is high, and circumstances prevent a clear definition or enforcement of property rights.[11] In turn, firms tend to perform worse than markets when they run poorly or are in monopoly situations without competition. According to Coase, net transaction costs drive the choice to exchange goods and services in a market or within a firm. The theory assumes that everyone involved will make rational decisions based on transparently available information and in consideration of all evidence. Against the backdrop of private property rights enforced by the state, neoclassical economic theory and modern political mythology cast markets or firms as the only ways to allocate goods and services effectively.

And yet political and economic theories are not necessarily true. Ostrom's first fundamental contribution to the study of CPRs was pointing out that Hardin's tragedy of the commons posed a problem in theory rather than in practice. She argued that the world was full of CPRs that—far from being tragedies—had been effectively managed and thriving for decades or centuries. In support, Ostrom drew together evidence from around the world. Her key cases involve the management of natural resources like water, timber, fish, or rangeland.

Research by Ostrom and her collaborators explained the "how" of CPR governance. In numerous papers and books, they documented the mechanisms that communities used to manage CPRs that did not rely on private property, prices, or bureaucratic hierarchies. Long-enduring common-property regimes rested on self-organized institutions of collective governance that had evolved in a bottom-up fashion and were executed among resource beneficiaries. Participants did not act out of the goodness of their hearts, or because they were restricted by custom and tradition. Rather, they upheld communal rights and duties out of "rational" prudence and self-interest.

The nonmarket, nonfirm, nonstate institutions developed to govern CPR exhibit striking diversity, and are tailored to the specific circumstances, resources, and people involved. Each resource requires specific management approaches for its particular character and natural

Participants did not act out of the goodness of their hearts. Rather, they upheld communal rights and duties out of "rational" prudence and self-interest.

environment. Fish and lobsters are free to move around, and often only seasonally available. Forests, by contrast, are quite literally rooted in a place and available to harvest continually. Although different in these common-property regimes' details, Ostrom maintained that they reflect broad "design principles." So while the nature of boundaries, access rights, rules, enforcement mechanisms, and monitoring arrangements differ, she suggested that some version of each would nearly always be present in successfully managed CPRs. Moreover, successful governance schemes coevolve in affinity with the surrounding social contexts.

But what kind of good is knowledge? In some sense, knowledge is a textbook case of a public good in that it is nonrival and nonexcludable. Once a piece of knowledge exists, everybody can have it. Many people can know about an idea, convey it to others, and use it without depletion. Even in material form, ideas can usually be replicated at low cost and without much effort. Beyond this, knowledge goods are rarely bound to a specific medium or carrier. These qualities fueled earlier knowledge revolutions of the printing press, electronic transmission, and broadcasting. They have become even more powerful with digital formats that are more easily copied and circulated. There is no risk of overconsumption or excessive appropriation. Digital knowledge goods can be copied and stored with perfect fidelity at a low cost.

Debates about global commons along with urgent economic and environmental challenges have provoked the application of these ideas beyond the types of natural resources Ostrom focused on. In recent years, people working in many domains have embraced the concepts of CPRs and commons, autonomous self-governance, and Ostrom's basic approach and design principles when thinking about knowledge. The commons concept has also been increasingly applied to networked telecommunications and knowledge. Indeed, Ostrom herself began exploring the idea of "knowledge as a commons" in a series of essays and an edited volume completed shortly before she died in 2012. For Ostrom and others, thinking of knowledge as a commons means a shift from a public goods framing focused merely on creating new knowledge goods to a CPR framing revolving around collective stewardship.[12]

And indeed, knowledge goods have become subject to legal and technical barriers to access that reflect enclosure. These barriers can be created and enforced through copyrights, patents, and various technical restrictions on file copying or transmission. While such restrictions are not tied to inherent features of the underlying good, they convert what would otherwise be a public good into something excludable. In doing so, technical and legal restrictions create artificial scarcity.

What purpose does the artificial scarcity of knowledge goods serve? Industrial policy and intellectual property law are typically justified in terms of a balance between public benefit and incentives for the production of new knowledge or creative works. Copyright, for example, provides the creator of a piece of expression—like a text, recording, song, or image—with certain exclusive rights to control or profit from the work, and sue anyone who violates these rights. Copyright restrictions create a temporary, legally enforced monopoly to encourage creators to pursue risky, uncertain work in the hopes that their efforts yield valuable outputs that could benefit them and society. Policymakers and state officials developed as well as imposed copyrights as a tool to align the incentives of creative individuals with the prosperity of nations. Consider that the authority to impose and enforce copyright restrictions was understood to be so profoundly important to national survival that it appears among the federal government's enumerated powers in Article I of the US Constitution.

Patents, centered on inventions as opposed to creative expression, differ in many details, but are similar in their fundamental goals. Patent holders also enjoy limited temporary monopolies. After the temporary period, the protected ideas and artifacts move into the public domain, where they are no longer subject to restrictions on use, adaptation, or dissemination. In this way, the law supports the expansion of a freely accessible public stock of knowledge that can be appropriated in future innovations and creative works.

Since the eighteenth century, however, when such laws first spread throughout Europe and beyond, the period of exclusive rights and privileges conferred by intellectual property laws has expanded enormously. What began as a few years of exclusive control first became a few dozen. In the latter half of the twentieth century, aggressive efforts to expand copyright terms led by commercial interests in the United States and Europe resulted in standard copyright terms of over a hundred years (usually codified in law as the authors' lifetime plus some fixed number of years). These terms were then standardized throughout much of the world in a series of international treaties. Such legal shifts have eroded the long-term value and collective benefits of public stocks of accessible, freely reusable knowledge goods in the service of enclosure and profit maximization. The era of copyright term extensions and "new enclosures" (a phrase coined by legal scholar James Boyle) over the second half of the twentieth century coincided with the rise of digital computing and communication technologies that make it easier and cheaper than ever to reproduce, share, and reuse knowledge-based and creative goods.[13] The result was an unstable tension between the proliferation of digitally networked knowledge commons and institutional regimes that restrict knowledge circulation by design.

In an influential critique of overly restrictive intellectual property rules, law professor Lawrence Lessig argued that tightened technological control and rampant regulation corrupt the generative vigor of the internet.[14] According to Lessig, the "creative" commons are burdened by exhaustive copyright constraints. Lessig enumerates three kinds of commons at stake. First, there is a commons of code, including software that runs the internet and was originally shared among developers. Second, there is a commons of knowledge (culture, ideas, and information about the world), the free exchange of which can be facilitated by the internet. Together, the commons of software and knowledge results in a commons of innovation. For Lessig, the internet affords technical and informational resources for innovation and creative engagement. Exaggerated protections that secure commercial exploitation, though, put this potential at risk. Such restrictions lose sight of the original idea of copyright. By foreclosing opportunities to share and remix freely, restrictive copyright shuts down the innovation commons. This has negative consequences for society's overall productive and creative capacity. Reduced access to knowledge leads to inefficiency and underutilization.

But with such powerful commercial forces arrayed against the growth and protection of accessible knowledge resources at the end of the twentieth century when Lessig wrote, what could be done? On what basis could a convincing alternative rooted in accessible and unrestricted commons be built?

By foreclosing opportunities to share and remix freely, restrictive copyright shuts down the innovation commons.

Geeks, Hackers, and Peers

In the December 7, 1972, issue of *Rolling Stone* magazine, interested readers found, amid news items about musician Carlos Santana and drug trafficking among hippies, a feature article about video games written by Stewart Brand and accompanied by photos taken by Annie Leibovitz. It introduced a world of "computer bums." These bums were mostly technicians and programmers employed in university and industry computing laboratories who engaged in combat with each other in a game called *Spacewar*. The "Spacewar Olympics" occurred in the evenings in a computer lab over a local network. But Brand's story not only revealed a colorful milieu of tech nuts idling away nighttime hours with beer and games in their office. It also highlighted the prospects of networked and computer-mediated communication for decentralized cooperation as well as the formation of social ties. The Spacewar Olympics demonstrated how microprocessors and electronic networks enabled people to connect, play, and collaborate in new and exciting ways. *Spacewar* had been created, shared, and improved through distributed collaboration over a precursor to the internet by programmers and engineers worldwide. Brand wrote, "When computers become available to everyone, the hackers take over. We are all Computer Bums, all more empowered as individuals and as co-operators. That might enhance things like the richness and the rigor of spontaneous creation and of human interaction, or sentient interaction."[15]

From the vantage point of a community of avid geeks, Brand urged his readers to envision what interconnected personal computers could do to improve the world. He assured them that protocols, wires, devices, and programs could become instruments for social connection, transformation, and empowerment.

When Brand published his piece on the Spacewar Olympics, visions and designs of the future "internetworked" computing tended to emphasize military, academic, and business uses. These visions reflected the priorities of the constellation of public and private actors involved in creating some of the first networking protocols in the early decades of the Cold War. These experiments included the Arpanet, which would evolve into the internet as we know it today. Investments in these new kinds of communications and computing infrastructure presumed that a resilient, interoperable, packet-based approach to internetworking, as it was known at the time, would offer a solid foundation for nascent computing and semiconductor industry growth as well as a strategic asset for the United States in the event of Soviet nuclear attack.[16]

Brand was a remarkable figure who straddled the military-industrial-academic world of cutting-edge technology and California counterculture scenes. After graduating from Stanford University, serving in the military, and studying art and design, Brand got involved in both scientific and recreational LSD experimentation along with multiple hippie and "back-to-the-land" communalist groups. Brand also joined the electrical engineering lab of Douglas Engelbart, a trailblazer of collaborative computing technologies credited with contributing to the invention of the mouse, windowing interfaces, hypertext, and version control systems. Brand embraced the DIY, futurist, and hacker ethos of these disparate social worlds. Between 1968 and 1971, he published the *Whole Earth Catalog*, a nearly broadsheet-sized, mixed-media periodical that promised like-minded readers "access to tools." The catalog promoted sundry utensils, implements, maps, and gizmos that might be useful for anyone hoping to run a commune, and espoused an ecologically and ethically minded vision of community building through rugged individualism. Readers included many who anticipated the potential of the new decentralized communication networks. Some were driven by an antiauthoritarian impetus, while others were drawn to the practical aspects of building a self-sufficient and autonomous life. Brand and his fellow travelers were laying the foundations of a culture of entrepreneurial, well-educated, and (almost exclusively) white and male leaders who embraced technology as a means for probing alternative ways to personal development, participatory democracy, and collectivity based on shared interests.

But California hippies and engineering elites like Brand were not the only ones experimenting with electronic communications systems in the booming postwar United States. Prior innovations in communications technologies combined with traditions of amateur tinkering had fed the rise of hobbyist technical communities. Ham, shortwave, and later citizens band radio enthusiasts gathered over the airwaves from backyard "shacks" or personal vehicles on the new interstate highways that crisscrossed the vast North American continent. Similarly, the monopolistic spread of the Bell telephone system birthed a fringe group of "phone phreaks" who found creative ways to reverse engineer administrative access into global telephonic networks and make calls anywhere they liked at zero cost. In one famous case, a phreaker prank called the Kremlin. The shrinking costs and sizes of semiconductors and other computing components inspired groups dedicated to "personal" microcomputers and software to run on them. Many of the participants in these hobbyist movements held day jobs in the growing computing and communications industries. Many were highly educated white men who, for one reason or another, struggled to connect or belong in other aspects of their lives. Most found joy, solidarity, or solace in the ability to talk shop, share ideas, and gain esteem among their fellow enthusiasts.[17]

Whatever brought them together, these hobbyist technology communities thrived in the 1960s and 1970s. They created magazines and social worlds with new traditions and cultures. They also generated numerous innovations that transformed society. Following a heavy blizzard in January 1978, Ward Christensen and Randy Seuss, both IBM employees and members of the Chicago Area Computer Hobbyists' Exchange, took advantage of the bad weather to work on a tool to make it easier for exchange members to communicate with each other. Combining a new file transfer protocol, some scraps of code, a spare computer, and a modulator-demodulator (now known as a "modem"), Christensen and Seuss created a digital answering machine and message exchange tool they called a "computerized bulletin board system," later shortened to BBS.

The "modem world" launched by the first Chicago BBS opened up new horizons of connectivity and interaction. Within a few years, community BBS systems popped up worldwide wherever phone lines and computing enthusiasts coexisted. These "boards" consisted of text-based, threaded discussions on prespecified topics. Constrained by the existing telephone infrastructure's geography (and costs), BBS communities combined disembodied anonymity and hyperlocal propinquity.[18] Many hosted thriving and diverse subcultures all of their own. Because Christensen and Seuss had freely shared the hardware specifications and source code for their system (in the tradition of hobbyist computing groups everywhere), extensions and improvements followed from others. The result was a patchwork of protocols that enabled new activities like distributed file sharing, electronic mail, and interactive gaming. The latter fulfilled the Spacewar Olympics fantasies that Brand had documented almost a decade earlier. On BBSs, almost two decades before the internet existed, thousands of people dialed in to exchange ideas, experiences, pornography, games, music, and more.

In 1985, Brand founded a BBS named after his catalog called the Whole Earth 'Lectronic Link (WELL) based out of Marin County, California. The WELL grew and thrived for over a decade. It attracted participants who, like Brand, shared communitarian social ideals, libertarian attitudes toward free speech, a fascination with digital technologies, and a penchant for building businesses that would make some of them spectacularly wealthy. Profound optimism about the transformative potential of technology underpinned all of these efforts. Around the same time, Brand worked with other *Whole Earth* adherents, computer experts, and hobbyists to convene the first Hackers' Conference (also in Marin County).[19] The event was partly a celebration of former *Whole Earth Catalog* author Stephen Levy's new book, *Hackers: Heroes of the Computer Revolution*.[20] Attendees included Steve Wozniak, the cofounder of Apple, Bob Wallace, one of Microsoft's first employees, and Ted Nelson, who coined the term "hypertext." Levy's book tried to spell out the norms and values that motivated the evolving community of software engineers, programmers, computer scientists, activists, and scholars who identified as hackers. The "hacker ethic," as Levy described it, emphasized technical proficiency, social transformation, and antiestablishment ideals. Sharing freely—both in a collaborative process of creative work and the products created—helped define what it meant to be a hacker. Skill and talent mattered more than formal authority, prestige, seniority, or credentials. Computers provided levers for cultural and artistic transformation, and were harbingers of a more open, cooperative society.

One attendee of the first Hackers' Conference who took the moral and ethical commitments of hacking more seriously than most was the young MIT computer scientist we met earlier, Stallman. As the printer story that opened this chapter illustrates, he rejected the growing commercialization of computer software. Having grown up with freely shared software, Stallman saw the emerging software industry as an enclosure of valuable knowledge commons in a way that paralleled the earlier enclosure and privatization of traditional natural commons. He envisioned a more collaborative and communal alternative.

Proprietary software, Stallman believed, destroyed computer users' freedoms to use their software in whatever ways they wanted, improve software when it didn't work the way they wanted, and share freely among hackers in a community. Stallman coined the term "free software" to describe software that supported these freedoms.[21] For Stallman, free software was an ethical imperative. His use of the term "free" was meant to invoke freedom, not price—something he expressed in the slogan that software should be "free as in free speech, not free beer." Because free software is also typically distributed at no price, some prefer the term "libre software."

By the end of the 1970s, one of the most widely used and highly respected operating systems in academia and industry was Unix. Developed at Bell Labs and initially distributed as free software, by the mid-1980s, Unix was, in effect, being slowly enclosed by large companies like IBM, HP, Digital, and Sun Microsystems—all of which had begun selling their proprietary operating systems based on the original Unix code. Recognizing this shift toward enclosure and ownership in software from his interactions with Xerox over the printer code, Stallman launched the GNU project in 1983. The term "GNU" stood for "GNU's Not Unix." The name was a nerdy joke on two levels. First, it evoked the programming trick of recursion by including "GNU" as the first term in the acronym expansion. Second, GNU sought to be Unix in all but name: it was a drop-in replacement for the increasingly proprietary operating system. Unlike Unix, however, it was to be built by a social movement committed to Stallman's vision of software freedom. In 1985, Stallman published "The GNU Manifesto"—a call to arms for free software.

To safeguard the accessibility, reuse, and modifiability of the GNU code he was writing from enclosure, Stallman looked to the formal institutions and law. In 1985, he created the nonprofit Free Software Foundation (FSF), which released several software licenses, most notably the GPL in 1989. The GPL enables users to inspect, change, and redistribute their software without permission. More important, it sought to prevent enclosure by stipulating that the core freedoms enshrined in the GPL must also be offered to others by anybody who redistributes either the GPL-licensed software or any other piece of software that builds on a piece of GPL-licensed code. The GPL is, for this reason, often described as viral: Any derivative of GPL-licensed software must be released under the GPL too. The effect is that the user of a piece of GPL-licensed software can do anything except withhold the freedoms they enjoy under the GPL from any downstream users.

In contrast to copyright, the viral principle embodied in the GPL is known as copyleft. It guarantees that the license perpetuates itself in the cumulative creative production process. Copyleft seeks to turn the freedom from proprietary encumbrances into a freedom for active participation. Under copyleft, people distributing creative work must let other users enjoy the same freedom to share, study, and modify the work. Ironically, the power to require this stems from copyright itself. Copyleft inverts copyright by turning an exclusive monopoly right to create scarcity into a requirement to keep things open and abundant.

Over the next decades, Stallman attracted thousands of people to the GNU project and FSF, where he served as president. These people contributed money, legal support, and—most of all—code. Although the movement's goal was the democratization of software production, it struggled to be inclusive. The people attracted to free software were overwhelmingly young, highly educated white men in Western countries with a science background and programming skills. Persistent gender disparities became a flash point, and in 2020, Stallman resigned from his position of FSF leadership after a pressure campaign called him out for a history of offensive behavior, interactions that caused women to feel uncomfortable, and controversial remarks about rape and underage sex. Stallman would later return to the FSF board of directors and remains a contentious figure today.

The GPL became a model for other frameworks that attempted to extend the idea of copyleft to creative domains beyond software. Foremost among these is the Creative Commons project created by Lessig in 2001. It offers a range of licenses—many of them copyleft—including those used for websites like Wikipedia, Stack Overflow, Fandom.com, and many more.

Although copyleft helped set the stage for peer production, it was fundamentally about creating knowledge commons and was not concerned with collaborative production. The success of the GNU operating system early on very much rested on Stallman's technical proficiency and dedication. In "The GNU Manifesto," Stallman even expressed skepticism that a high-quality operating system could be built collaboratively. In the late 1980s and 1990s, the FSF hired software developers to build GNU.

Others, however, would find ways to write operating systems more collaboratively. A twenty-one-year-old computer science student in Helsinki, Finland, Linus Torvalds learned of and got excited about the GNU project from afar. Torvalds started prototyping a critical operating system component called a kernel that acts as the central command processor. Kernel writing is considered difficult technical work, and the lack of a kernel was among the most glaring pieces missing from Stallman's GNU project in the early 1990s. Instead of trying to complete the GNU-compatible kernel by himself, Torvalds released the source code of an early version on a public file-sharing server and invited contributions to the project. One of the server administrators nicknamed the project Linux—a portmanteau of Torvalds's first name and Unix. Others combined Torvalds's new kernel with the rest of the GNU system and the project exploded in popularity. Although the combined system is typically called Linux, it is more accurately described as GNU/Linux. Torvalds's work inspired others to get involved in building the Linux kernel. With so many helping hands, subsequent releases of Linux improved rapidly. Several of the first Linux operating system distributions were released within a year.[22]

To manage the piecemeal input from a loose group of people, Torvalds had to develop procedures for making decisions and coordinating contributions. Creating Linux was therefore both a technological challenge and complex social task. Torvalds assumed the role of a "benevolent dictator" for his project, deciding which new features or bug fixes made it into the system, and coordinating the software releases. Other features for tracking bugs, archiving patches, and communication were also created and installed.

While Torvalds had control over the Linux kernel, none of the other contributors were his employees. As a result, Torvalds could accept or reject a patch to the Linux software, but he could not allocate resources or order people to do things like a manager in a more traditional software firm. Contributors to Linux could always choose not to participate, to leave, or even to make a copy of the code and take it in a new direction (this is frequently referred to as a "fork" in the software development community). Torvalds's authority rested on the respect and compliance of his peers. His management activities involved making suggestions, giving feedback, and sometimes erupting in long, toxic rants over public email lists to pressure others to accept his vision. Implicitly, Torvalds trusted that a large base of users and codevelopers would ultimately find and fix any errors in Linux. This idea became known as "Linus's law," a term coined by software developer Eric S. Raymond: "Given enough eyeballs, all bugs are shallow."

In 1997, Raymond first published an essay titled *The Cathedral and the Bazaar* that encapsulated his experiences with and understanding of Linux development. He argued that the model was a more generally useful production method and not just some idiosyncratic feature of Torvalds or his project.[23] Raymond likened the process to constructing a bazaar, in which the creation of code happens in a chaotic bottom-up process where participants build little pieces here and there, the combination of which becomes greater than the sum of the parts. He contrasted this with the traditional, corporate, top-down software development method, which he compared to building a cathedral. Raymond asserted that by allowing for the mass aggregation of small contributions from diversely motivated developers working outside managerial hierarchies, Stallman's free software movement could create software that was not merely as good as proprietary software but instead better.

Because Raymond felt Stallman's talk about social movements and user freedom was not sufficiently business friendly, he worked with other free software leaders to coin a new term: "open source." At its core, open source software was just another phrase for free software. The original open source definition, for example, was simply a copy of an existing free software definition with the term "free software" swapped out for "open source." That said, open source reflected a way of arguing for free software by de-emphasizing that code would be made publicly available and talking up the fact that making code available would lead to better software. As noted earlier, many people today refer to free or open source software using the amalgamation "free/libre open source software."

Raymond's writing was influential and convinced Netscape Corporation to release the source code of its Navigator web browser. This release became the Mozilla project, eventually producing the Firefox web browser and Thunderbird email client. Other FLOSS initiatives like the Apache web server and MySQL database management system became early market leaders while being developed collaboratively and in commons. Together with a host of other free software solutions, they shape the everyday experience of countless people using digital media and networked services. This success has a commercial side. For instance, when shares of VA Linux Systems (now Geeknet), a business selling computers installed with Linux, opened for trading on December 9, 1999, the company broke the record for the largest first-day gain in stock price as it rose from $30 to $239.25 per share. VA Linux, along with other companies like RedHat Software, became poster children of the dot-com boom and brought FLOSS business models into the mainstream of the software industry.

The widespread adoption of FLOSS tools like GNU/Linux, Apache, and MySQL, combined with the spectacular profits of companies like VA Linux, signaled a sea change. Torvalds and Stallman had stumbled on something radical and new: the technical, legal, social, and psychological mechanisms for a novel, decentralized means of producing public knowledge goods. The GNU/Linux systems they built were the world's introduction to commons-based peer production and what it could do. GNU/Linux and other projects like it combined distributed collaboration in autonomous, volunteer communities via personal computers over the internet to create as well as manage complex knowledge goods released under copyleft licenses.

FLOSS also inspired other kinds of collaborative endeavors. Stallman himself wrote in a 1999 essay that the GNU/Linux might be adapted to create an online encyclopedia in the FLOSS model. Wikipedia was founded by Jimmy Wales and Larry Sanger two years later. At the Ames Laboratory of the US National Aeronautics and Space Administration in late 2000, a small team tasked with labeling thousands of images of craters on the surface of Mars put out an open call for help via the web. Volunteers showed up and submitted hundreds of thousands of labels that in the aggregate, matched the quality of those provided by professional scientists with doctorates. Across diverse domains—peer-to-peer file-sharing networks, distributed computing, digital mapping, news filtering, and others—online communities of amateurs, volunteers, and hobbyists working collaboratively seemed to sprout like weeds.

Yochai Benkler saw the transformative potential of these new modes of distributed online collaboration earlier than most. In a 2002 essay, he coined the term, as mentioned earlier, "commons-based peer production" to describe the nascent model of collaborative organization. In the piece, Benkler drew from Coase's transaction cost theory to argue that peer production had emerged because the internet had driven the transaction costs associated with coordination and cooperation so incredibly low that it was now easier to do something cooperatively than it was to contract on the market or hire somebody within a firm.[24] In his 2006 book *The Wealth of Networks*, Benkler brought together economics, law, and political philosophy to provide a scholarly account of how something like Linux worked, what it meant for traditional thinking about technology and society, and what impacts it might create.[25] He envisioned peer production in an expansive light: The radical possibility to collaborate remotely over the internet outside market-based transactions and managerial hierarchies heralded a new networked knowledge economy. In Benkler's telling, peer production would transform the world.

With several decades of hindsight, the early 2000s look like a high-water mark for peer production hype, and

The radical possibility to collaborate remotely over the internet outside market-based transactions and managerial hierarchies heralded a new networked knowledge economy.

aspects of Benkler's argument feel utopian. Nevertheless, much of the transformative potential of peer production that Benkler predicted has been realized in ways that we will elaborate throughout the rest of this book. Today, for instance, concepts and practices innovated in peer production have influenced the evolution of social media and the web, blockchain, biohacking, political activism, and the maker movement. Likewise, scholarly and public inquiry into the organization, culture, and effects of peer production have expanded enormously. These shifting currents spring from the intertwined histories of computing and virtual communities that made peer production and the internet what they are at present. They also reflect the deeper roots of peer production that predate the social web by several centuries.

3

IMPACT: WHAT HAS PEER PRODUCTION ACHIEVED?

Nearly all accounts of peer production—including this book—open by invoking some of its most visible achievements. In this chapter, we take stock of these achievements in a more in-depth way. Some of peer production's impacts are relatively easy to list, such as the creation of particular valuable information resources or software. But peer production has also had less direct impacts that are harder to measure. Part of peer production's value stems from the benefits to its participants and contributors. The result is a world deeply shaped by peer production along with its products and processes.

Valuable Peer Produced Resources

As we described in chapter 2, FLOSS was the first example of peer production. To this day, FLOSS remains peer production's greatest and most visible success. The GNU/Linux operating system is widely used in various applications across the computing sector. Many immediately think of personal desktop and laptop computers when they hear "operating systems." Surprisingly, personal computing is one of the few parts of the computing sector that is not dominated by peer produced operating systems. Today, the Linux kernel runs on over a third of embedded systems (such as the in-flight entertainment systems on major airlines), large mainframe computers used in businesses, and servers that run the web. The most extreme example of Linux's dominance is supercomputers. According to the TOP500 project, which tracks and ranks supercomputers globally, GNU/Linux-based systems went from 0 percent market share before 1998 to 100 percent by 2017. Most general-purpose computers also run Linux-based operating systems today simply because most computing devices shipped worldwide are smartphones, and most smartphones have run Android since 2015.[1] The Android operating system runs on a branch of the Linux kernel. Trends in market share over time suggest that peer produced kernels and operating systems are not facing short-term threats to their dominance.

That said, an operating system is just the substrate on which one runs applications. Other peer produced FLOSS run on top of peer produced operating systems like GNU/Linux and Android. For example, web servers are the applications that retrieve and then distribute web pages when people enter a site address in their browsers. Every website uses a web server, making them crucial and widespread tools. Apache—which got its name because it was "a patchy" web server made up of a range of bug fixes and features (i.e., "patches") assembled through peer production—has dominated web server rankings for almost as long as records have been kept. When it eventually gave up its throne in 2019, it was to nginx—another peer produced FLOSS web server.

Web browsers are another domain where peer produced FLOSS has thrived, although sometimes in less visible ways. Netscape Navigator was one of the first commercial proprietary software applications to be spun out from a company and released as FLOSS. While Netscape is gone today, Firefox, the peer produced browser built from the codebase that Netscape released, lives on. Its major competitors—Google Chrome, Apple Safari, and Microsoft Edge—are all based on a different system called Webkit, which is itself based on a peer produced web browser core that originated in the FLOSS KDE desktop project.

Several decades ago, Oracle built a fortune on its eponymous proprietary database. Over time, its market share was whittled away by FLOSS competitors like MySQL and PostgreSQL. Similarly, many of the most important programming languages today are peer-produced. For instance, Perl, Python, Ruby, and PHP are all FLOSS projects created by volunteers. Each language has been adopted by the largest technology companies in the world: early versions of the Amazon website were built in Perl; Facebook used PHP; Instagram used Python; and Twitter used Ruby. Other languages like JavaScript, Java, Go, and Rust were created by large organizations and released as FLOSS. In different parts of the software industry, each has gained competitive market share—if not dominance—through improvements and development driven by peer production as users contribute back. Other languages like C, C++, Java, and R exist in both proprietary and peer produced forms. Over time, the peer produced versions of each have grown to dominate many, and often most, of their respective markets.

These examples only scratch the surface. Small pieces of peer produced software have taken on outsized roles too, such as a little tool called OpenSSL. The "SSL" in the name stands for "secure socket layer" and describes how the system encrypts internet connections. OpenSSL does that one little thing, but it does it so well that it is the foundation of most secure web connections, many virtual private networks, most secure email connections, and so on. If you have seen a lock icon in your browser, the connection was likely protected by OpenSSL.

These examples illustrate how peer produced software has become critical digital infrastructure that is ubiquitous and relied on by an enormous number of other tools, individuals, and organizations. When you view a web page, you typically use dozens of pieces of peer produced software to communicate with other pieces of peer produced software over peer produced network infrastructure. We may not see or even know about the role of peer production in these systems, but it is everywhere, and we rely on it constantly.

The realm of digital infrastructure points to another area where peer production has made a major impact: the creation and distribution of knowledge bases. Like internet infrastructure, knowledge bases are difficult to touch or see directly. They encompass collections of various information goods that people rely on for various reasons. Today, peer production dominates the domain of knowledge bases. This is largely thanks to another familiar example: Wikipedia.

Wikipedia might be peer production's model organism. It is among the largest peer production communities measured by volunteer contributors and is probably the most well-known. It is also the most widely studied peer production project. The academic search engine Google Scholar identifies almost 25,000 articles with Wikipedia in the title. The English Wikipedia has more than 7 million articles, revised more than 1.3 billion times by as of October 2025. Many English Wikipedia articles contain detailed information, including more than 6,800 "Featured" articles, which are meticulously sourced and among the most comprehensive reference works on their subjects.

Articles in English Wikipedia tend to be high quality. In an influential 2008 study published in *Nature*, Jim Giles gave a sample of 42 Wikipedia and *Encyclopædia Britannica* articles on the same subjects to a group of experts to evaluate (without telling them which article came from which source).[2] The Wikipedia and *Encyclopædia Britannica* articles both had errors, and the Wikipedia articles had no more "serious" errors than the *Encyclopædia Britannica* write-ups. Since then, this kind of comparison has been repeated dozens of times for many topics. Several have focused on medical information and comparisons with textbooks, where the consequences of incorrect information are particularly high. In general, Wikipedia articles have been shown to be at least as high quality as some of the best and highest-quality reference works in print. Moreover, they are at least on par with other widely used knowledge bases on the web that are the realistic alternatives.

To be clear, the "encyclopedia anyone can edit" contains numerous errors and is vandalized constantly. People often add vulgarity or misinformation to Wikipedia articles. Wikipedia's openness, though, means that such damage is typically reverted quickly—frequently within seconds by volunteer-created software called "bots"—before anybody sees it. The result is that Wikipedia is at least as comprehensive, reliable, high quality, and well referenced as alternatives, and is revised much more quickly. Wikipedia is now widely seen as the best publicly available source of reliable knowledge. For example, when Google came under pressure for misinformation being propagated on YouTube, its executives publicly suggested that they would link to Wikipedia articles on the topics of articles from misleading YouTube videos on similar subjects.[3]

While Wikipedia's superiority in quality over nonpeer produced alternatives might be debatable, its superiority in quantity is a settled matter. Wikipedia is, without question, the largest and most comprehensive general-purpose reference work ever created. In some cases, English Wikipedia has better coverage than specialist reference works. Because it is edited by volunteers, Wikipedia can be up to date in ways that traditional reference works cannot. Famously, English Wikipedia reported that US singer Michael Jackson died more than fifty minutes before his death was officially confirmed. As University of Colorado professor Brian Keegan and coauthors have documented, English Wikipedia has collected and integrated breaking news coverage on events like airplane crashes and natural disasters rapidly as well as effectively.[4]

Of course, English Wikipedia is only the largest version of Wikipedia. Wikipedia exists in more than 300 different language editions. Combined, these versions have more than 65 million article pages. Almost 20 different language Wikipedia editions have more than 1 million articles.[5] Although some of these articles begin as translations from the English version, the vast majority develop independently so that they highlight the most relevant information for readers in a given language. Smaller Wikipedias have received far less attention from researchers, but they are particularly important because the languages themselves are often underresourced in terms of numbers of speakers or volumes of published materials. Wikipedia usually provides the best reference material available for these underresourced languages.

Wikipedia pages are viewed more than 15 billion times monthly across all language editions as of October 2025. Wikipedia has been among the top 10 most visited web pages since at least 2008, typically ranked fifth or sixth. This is even though Wikipedia is blocked in some of the world's most populous countries—most famously, the People's Republic of China. For millions of people each day, Wikipedia is a source of answers to questions, guide to homework, arbiter of disagreements, and news source. It is also, as we will elaborate later, a foundational source of training data for generative AI systems such as large language models (LLMs) like OpenAI's ChatGPT.

Wikipedia's success has completely dominated and transformed the encyclopedia industry. While it did not start with the aim to bring down the existing world of encyclopedias, it fundamentally challenged and finally upended their model of operation. For the most part, general-purpose encyclopedias relied on the sale of expensive multivolume editions. The production cycle was long, with new editions coming out only after decades of writing, revision, and editing, all in the hands of a small group of experts. In 2012, the *Encyclopædia Britannica* ceased print production, and publishers of reference works in other languages have followed suit.

And this is just Wikipedia. There is a huge variety of other peer produced wikis online. In 2004, for example, one of Wikipedia's cofounders and several core contributors started a for-profit company called Wikia (mostly rebranded as Fandom.com since 2016) to host peer produced wikis on any topic. The site used much of the same technical and social infrastructure as Wikipedia, and over 20 years later, it has hosted more than 385,000 wikis on numerous subjects. Many of these are special-purpose collections of knowledge and information that go beyond the scope of a more "traditional" encyclopedic project like Wikipedia. For instance, in science fiction fan media, Wookieepedia is an encyclopedia that hosts more than 190,000 pages about *Star Wars*. Similarly, Memory Alpha is an encyclopedia with more than 57,000 pages about *Star Trek*. The largest Fandom wikis tend to focus on fan culture, but others collect information about, say, the city of Seattle, academic jobs, video games, cancer, and much more. Although less well-known than Wikipedia, Fandom is regularly ranked among the top 25 websites in the world.[6]

And this is just wikis. Over time, peer production knowledge bases have branched far beyond wikis. For example, enormous Q&A sites like Quora, the (now defunct) Yahoo Answers, and the Stack Exchange network of communities all rely on peer produced content. On these sites, individuals post their questions publicly. Anyone else can view these questions and provide answers. Through this simple process, peer produced Q&A projects have created several of the largest and highest-quality question-driven knowledge bases anywhere. The most well-known Stack Exchange community, Stack Overflow, revolves around computer programming Q&A, and offers unparalleled, widely used resources for learning and working programmers.

Maps are another kind of knowledge base that peer production has excelled at building. The OpenStreetMap project has created peer produced maps that are competitive with Google Maps in many locations. The maps include data on both streets and paths along with "points of interest" like parks or restaurants with details such as opening hours. Ever see a map on an in-flight entertainment system? Odds are the underlying data came from OpenStreetMap. Within the OpenStreetMap community, there are rail fans who contribute information about trains, hikers who contribute information about trails, and so on. The Humanitarian OpenStreetMap project has created detailed street maps from satellite images in the face of natural disasters like hurricanes and earthquakes to help route emergency workers in stricken contexts.

The foregoing examples illustrate some of the highest-impact peer production knowledge bases. Several of these resources are visited or accessed billions of times every day, whether or not consumers of the information realize that they rely on peer production. Still, other valuable peer production resources and approaches are even less visible. These include areas that require the aggregation of knowledge about relevance or importance. Such knowledge is, by definition, diffuse and distributed across many people. While predigital information ecosystems all had mechanisms for finding and separating crucial bits from everything else, many of these systems relied on the editorial judgment of experts. Peer production innovated ways of curating information at a much faster pace and vastly larger scale by, in most cases, bypassing experts entirely.

Indirect Uses and Impacts

So far, our story of peer production's impact has concentrated on direct effects—that is, the information artifacts produced directly by the peers. Many of peer production's largest impacts are indirect. These can be more difficult to grasp or attribute to peer production, but are perhaps even more striking. For instance, the number of Wikipedia page views—as eye-popping as it might be—vastly underestimates Wikipedia's reach. If you search on Google

Peer production innovated ways of curating information at a much faster pace and vastly larger scale by, in most cases, bypassing experts entirely.

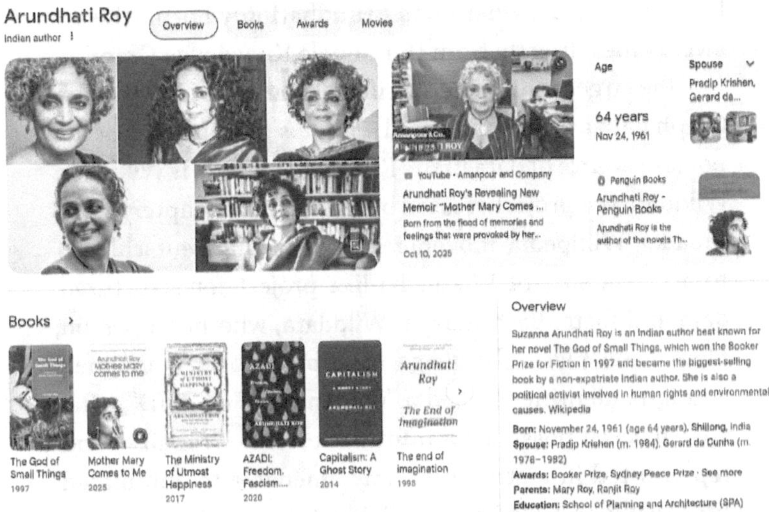

Figure 1 Google search results example from March 2026. Notice that the "Overview" text block on the right-hand side and the first link appearing on the bottom left are both to Wikipedia. The cards along the top also incorporate facts (Roy's age and her spouse's name), likely drawn directly from Wikidata, a peer produced knowledge base.

for "Arundhati Roy" as shown in figure 1, Google will answer basic questions about her directly. It will also often provide a sidebar to search results that show basic facts about the topic. This sidebar is called the Google Knowledge Graph, and the facts are aggregated (automatically by Google servers) from several places on the web. When someone attempts to search Google using a voice query like “OK Google, where was Arundhati Roy born,” the answer comes directly from the Google Knowledge Graph.

The largest and most significant sources of Knowledge Graph data are peer produced. Perhaps the single most important source of data in the Knowledge Graph is Wikidata. Wikidata is a project created by the German chapter of the broader Wikipedia movement (Wikimedia Deutschland) to act as a sort of Wikipedia-like project for structured data and facts. Each item in Wikidata, whether a person, place, book, planet, language, concept, or so on, is assigned a unique identifier (called a “Q identifier” or “QID”). The QID makes it possible for information to be organized and represented in a structured way amenable to automated processing and retrieval. Individual items might possess properties that help identify them as part of a larger set. For instance, the Wikidata item corresponding to Arundhati Roy (QID 212801) could be assigned properties corresponding to being a woman, writer, political activist, and person born in Shillong, India. It could also include appropriate spellings of her name in languages that do not use a Latin alphabet, connections to titles of her books, awards she has received, and so forth. These properties and items can then be aggregated, organized, and queried in multiple languages, resulting in reliable Google Knowledge Graph infobox material that accompanies search results.

The value of Wikidata is immense. Even if you've only ever read Wikipedia articles in a single language, consider that Wikidata can encompass the scope of all the articles in all the language editions of Wikipedia as well as all the things and ideas in the world that Wikipedia editors have collected and curated information about. In addition, the contents of Wikidata, like Wikipedia and its other sister projects, are licensed to allow free access and reuse by anyone in the world. For a company like Google, whose original mission was "to organize the world's information and make it universally accessible and useful," Wikidata is a windfall—structured, detailed, multilingual, and human-curated data of greater breadth than probably any other single source. Google even hired Croatian computer scientist Denny Vrandečić, one of the designers and cofounders of Wikidata, to work on the Google Knowledge Graph (he has since returned to Wikimedia).

Many knowledge bases exist that are similar to the Google Knowledge Graph. Like Google, many of the most widely used draw from Wikidata and other peer produced knowledge bases. Virtual personal assistants like Amazon's Alexa, Microsoft's Cortana, and Apple's Siri pull their data from the web, Wikidata, and other peer produced sources, even though they usually do not attribute their source clearly. The fact that peer produced knowledge bases are so large, high quality, and freely available makes them the obvious starting point for a Knowledge Graph. Researchers at Apple, for example, have published papers on clever techniques they have created for extracting factoids from unstructured data in Wikipedia articles and other peer produced knowledge bases. If it feels like these virtual assistants know everything, it's because they draw from the freely available knowledge bases created by peer production.

In some ways, the link between search engines and peer production is stronger than our description implies. Research led by Isaac Johnson and colleagues at Northwestern University has shown that Google is enormously dependent on Wikipedia.[7] The team had a series of volunteer study participants modify their web browser in a way that—unbeknownst to the subjects participating in the study—scrubbed search results of any links and factoids that were obviously taken from Wikipedia. The research team found a symbiotic relationship between Wikipedia and Google. A huge portion of Google's ability to provide people with answers to the questions they searched for was a function of Wikipedia content showing up at the top of their search results. According to the researchers, more than one-third of successful searches (judging from click-through rates) could be attributed to the presence of Wikipedia. Because Wikipedia is only one peer produced knowledge base, this is likely a huge underestimate of peer production's importance.

Peer production has had effects in the world beyond the internet too. Once again, the model organism Wikipedia has provided some of the clearest examples. Take

If it feels like these virtual assistants know everything, it's because they draw from the freely available knowledge bases created by peer production.

a working paper study by Neil Thompson and Douglas Hanley that describes an experiment where graduate students in chemistry were paid to write new articles about important topics in their field that were missing from Wikipedia.[8] Thompson and Hanley published a random subset of those articles on English Wikipedia and withheld the other half until later. They found strong evidence that the scientific literature in chemistry began to shift based on the articles they had uploaded. The presence of specific articles on Wikipedia caused the authors of published articles in the scientific literature to talk about topics in particular ways. They also found that citations to articles included in the Wikipedia articles increased. In another case, a group of economists ran an experiment in which they expanded a set of Wikipedia articles (across multiple language editions) about a random subset of small towns in Spain.[9] They left another set of towns' articles unchanged as a control group. The towns assigned to receive a better Wikipedia article experienced increased tourism as measured in subsequent hotel bookings and tourism revenue compared to the control group. Peer production has a real impact on things in the world.

Peer produced knowledge bases supply freely licensed raw materials for an enormous amount of follow-on research as well. For instance, entire fields of computational linguistics rely on peer produced sources. Once again, the massive and multilingual Wikipedia leads the way. Thousands of papers in natural language processing, computational linguistics, and information retrieval mine Wikipedia data sources and other peer produced knowledge bases. Natural language processing, like machine learning and AI, in general, relies on large training datasets to "teach" algorithms to classify data, generate new data, and act intelligently. Take a simple example of an AI system designed to tell the difference between pictures of dogs and cats (similar functionality is built into many photo-sharing apps). This system would be trained using a large amount of "labeled data"—in other words, pictures of dogs and cats that have been categorized correctly already. After this training, the algorithm is then shown new pictures, and then can generate a "guess" about whether each one should fall into the "dog" or "cat" categories that it was trained to recognize. Although an enormous amount of work goes into developing great algorithms, even the best AI algorithm is completely useless until it "learns" from a large pile of cases. As part of this learning process, the algorithm associates which combination of clues can distinguish between the relevant categories. Because peer production knowledge bases are vast, freely licensed, and widely accessible, they form the data backbone that makes many of the most successful AI systems work.

Since late 2022, when OpenAI first released a public version of ChatGPT, generative LLMs have become synonymous with AI. LLMs now represent the state of the art for many AI and machine learning tasks, including machine translation, annotation, and various simulations. While the details of the training data along with the code used to create or update the LLMs are frequently not public, and certainly not produced through peer production, they all rely on troves of public training data from peer produced knowledge bases and communities. For instance, one of Microsoft's core generative AI products, Copilot, provides working snippets and autocompletion for software code and programmers. It is not a coincidence that Microsoft also owns the widely used software repository hosting site GitHub, the largest hosting service for FLOSS projects and the primary source of training data for Copilot. LLMs typically give higher weights to some data sources than others, and nearly all public LLMs treat Wikipedias as the among the most highly weighted sources. They supplied an enormous trove of texts and factual information in many different languages that was used to train LLMs. High-profile licensing contracts between AI firms and peer production community hosting sites like Stack Exchange underscore that peer production is a crucial resource that underpins AI. Part of the growth and success of machine learning and AI systems over the last several years can be attributed to the wide availability of public training data from peer produced knowledge bases. Several generative

AI projects have also adopted an open model of cooperation along the lines of peer production.

Benefits to Participants

A less appreciated impact of peer production is the way it benefits participants. For many contributors, peer production is enjoyable and empowering, can build valuable skills, and may even support the development of virtue. In his essay *The Cathedral and the Bazaar*, Raymond argued that FLOSS participants were "scratching their own itch"—that is, contributing to projects because they benefited from doing so. In Raymond's telling, people fix bugs in FLOSS because the bugs affect them, and they share the fixes with others because it is cheap to do so (i.e., because of low transaction costs). People released their software as FLOSS in the first place because it meant that a crowd might help maintain the software—an expensive and time-intensive process. As we will explain in chapter 4, Raymond's itch-scratching model is far from a complete account of how FLOSS works. But it does point to a real set of individual-level impacts of FLOSS in particular and peer production more generally. Peer production also happens because participants derive fun, satisfaction, and enjoyment. For activities like mapmaking or encyclopedia writing, most people simply could not pursue them before peer production. Additionally, peer production is deeply social. To the extent that peer production helps people connect and build interpersonal bonds, it improves their lives too.

Insofar as peer production helps people transcend their roles as consumers of knowledge to become producers, peer production empowers participants as well. Take the technical infrastructure of communication. Increasingly, our communication is mediated by cell phones and personal computing devices. Under these circumstances, control over these technologies is control over our experience. If one relies on a series of devices and networks to contact one's family, friends, or coworkers, the question of who makes and manages those devices and networks has deep political implications. By returning some control over their technological infrastructure, peer production can empower people to shape their own experiences of the world. If my software is not working as I want, I can (in theory) change it, but only if it is FLOSS. Similar arguments can be made about other kinds of information and cultural goods. Peer production renders knowledge artifacts something that anyone can produce, revise, improve, and share—rather than something you can only consume as is.

Linked to this empowerment idea, several city, regional, and even national governments have adopted and

By returning some control over their technological infrastructure, peer production can empower people to shape their own experiences of the world.

invested in peer production to advance their sovereignty and autonomy. In the early 2000s, regions in Spain, including Extremadura and Valencia, created special versions of GNU/Linux-based operating systems to ensure that citizens and the government were not dependent on foreign-owned multinational companies. In some cases, they took advantage of this to ensure that the software was localized into regional languages in ways that would not have made financial sense for large companies. For languages like Catalan, Welsh, and Icelandic, where most computer users are skilled in "major" languages like Spanish or English, the localization of software or reference works often does not yield profits for a company. Will Microsoft sell more copies if it translates Windows into Welsh? Probably not. With peer production, people who care—volunteers or those paid by the government—can step up and translate without permission.

Making similar arguments about the need for local control, municipal governments in Munich and Barcelona, state governments in the Indian state of Kerala and Brazilian state of Rio Grande do Sul, and national governments in Brazil, South Korea, and Croatia have all adopted FLOSS. Moreover, Uruguay distributed laptops from the One Laptop per Child project to all schoolchildren in the country as part of its Project Ceibal effort. Because One Laptop per Child was built on peer produced FLOSS infrastructure, Project Ceibal took over most parts of the development of both client and server infrastructure to provide children in Uruguay with the kind of education that the Uruguayan government wanted. When One Laptop per Child itself struggled, Project Ceibal was able to continue. As well, the use of FLOSS meant that project reflected the policies and needs of Uruguay better than any off-the-shelf alternative that a company like Microsoft might have provided.

In the process of creating things, participants in peer production build valuable skills. FLOSS, for example, gives opportunities to participate in making software to anybody with an internet connection. By writing software with others, participants can learn in an environment with relatively low stakes and few barriers. Several decades after FLOSS's ascendance, there is a long list of professional software developers who cut their teeth as volunteers in FLOSS projects. It is now normal to find participation in FLOSS projects on software engineering résumés. Prospective employers of software engineers routinely ask for records of public contributions to FLOSS code repositories. When hiring a developer, it can be difficult to understand if someone has the skills to build a specific type of software without looking at the things they have created. For developers with experience in FLOSS, evidence of their skills is already in public and ready to be inspected by potential employers.

Contributing to peer production creates a public record of work that also can result in public recognition.

Today, the lead developers of widely used peer production projects are among the most respected programmers worldwide and most frequent keynote speakers at technical conferences. Similarly excellent work on proprietary software within a large company, although just as difficult, is less visible. Contributing to the most widely used FLOSS projects is hard to match in terms of impact too. Dutch programmer Guido van Rossum founded the peer produced programming language Python, discussed above, and has been hired into a series of high-profile positions at Google, Dropbox, and Microsoft. In each case, the hiring set off a wave of news coverage and generated goodwill for the company. Similarly, there are Geographic Information System professionals who learned their trade on OpenStreetMap, professional copy editors who learned the ropes with Project Gutenberg's distributed proofreaders, and so on. Indeed, many examples scattered throughout this book involve projects created by volunteers who built expertise and skills before transitioning into full-time employment supporting their peer production projects.

Of course, participants in peer production learn about much more than just techniques and skills related to knowledge production. Peer production involves coordination with complex, distributed teams, high levels of cooperation, digital media literacies, and more. Participation in peer production builds most of these skills, and in a world that relies on peer produced resources, reflects an important skill in and of itself.

Peer production may even build virtue by allowing people to act in ways emphasizing cooperation, sharing, and helping strangers. This argument, made by Benkler and philosopher Helen Nissenbaum, emphasizes how some people acting generously by contributing to peer production projects can set off a virtuous cycle, shaping how those involved think of themselves.[10] Recent empirical research, including papers by economist Jérôme Hergueux and colleagues, finds a correlation between the degree to which people contribute to peer production projects like FLOSS and Wikipedia, and the extent to which they act in prosocial, cooperative, and altruistic ways in other settings.[11] Perhaps by providing viable, cooperative alternatives to more hierarchical and market-driven organizing models, peer production allows some participants to embrace their better angels and act more generously.

A World Shaped by Peer Production

Maybe the largest and most important way that peer production has affected the world has little to do with peer production itself. Peer production has inspired a range of things that borrow features of peer production and apply them elsewhere.

Several major peer production projects that emerged in the late 1990s and early 2000s coincided with the dot-com boom along with the rise of companies like Amazon, Google, and eBay. Following a market collapse between 2001 and 2003, the venture-funded tech sector regrouped around a vision of web-based businesses powered by social, participatory, and user-generated content. The results of this shift came to be known as "Web 2.0," and gave rise to many of today's most popular websites and services. Facebook (2004), YouTube (2005), and Twitter (2006) all came online during this era. Apple released the first-generation iPhone in 2007, ushering in the smartphone era. The digital economy pivoted rapidly, powered by advertising and insights mined from vast troves of user activity data. The business models at the heart of this shift offer integral examples of what management scholar Shoshana Zuboff terms "surveillance capitalism," in which the most valuable commodity is the attention of the billions of users of global, web-scale platforms.[12]

Web users differ from traditional media audiences. Instead of simply consuming content created by broadcasters, studios, and publishers, people have come together online to create, exchange, and organize vast quantities of media themselves. In many cases, web users have also produced the ratings, reviews, and metadata that can help platforms deploy algorithmic systems to sort as well as rank things to maximize the number and duration of views. Such exchanges inspired the creation of new systems for the peer-to-peer provision of goods and services. Companies like Airbnb, Uber, UpWork, and OnlyFans stepped in as marketplaces and intermediaries of short-term contracting in various domains. Decentralized "Web 3.0" tools powered by blockchain and related technologies push toward decentralized production. Although these platforms deviate from peer production in important ways (see our definition and discussion early in chapter 1), peer production communities trailblazed many of the underlying social and technological systems involved.

An excellent example comes from what is sometimes called, as noted already, the sharing economy. An earlier generation of peer produced projects like Couchsurfing and Hospitality Club allowed for "network hospitality" through which people could connect with strangers to stay in each other's homes for free when traveling. These sites were built on similar, preinternet arrangements coordinated through catalogs. As online communities, the sites developed novel reputation systems that relied on networks of references and reviews to enable their members to trust strangers enough to invite them into their homes and enter others' homes when invited. Over time, a similar model was adapted by a series of private, frequently venture-funded companies. Most famously, Airbnb integrated the same basic reputation mechanisms into a site, creating a market for the same basic service. To be clear,

Airbnb is not peer production, but it built a market for short-term accommodations on the same tools for managing reputations and trust that peer production communities had proven could work. We return to this case in the final part of our book.

A similar pattern played out among "ride-sharing" companies like Uber, Lyft, Didi, Grab, and others. The companies create markets and technical tools that enable individuals to offer as well as request rides at a far greater scale and reduced cost compared to traditional taxi firms. In doing so, they often provide vast improvements over many earlier transportation services (even as they frequently fail to offer living wages or sustainable working conditions for drivers). As with Airbnb, these were inspired by and built on community-based models of cooperative resource management innovated by peer production communities. Their core business models harness small contributions distributed across many people coordinated remotely over digital communications networks. Sound familiar?

Another illustration comes from what some dub "collaborative filtering." The process of aggregating many small suggestions about the relevance, importance, or value of any information good is yet another domain where peer production has excelled. Effective collaborative filtering systems make it possible to sift through enormous streams of knowledge in almost any form (new stories, pictures, videos, tweets, and so on) and identify examples that meet almost any criteria. Early collaborative filtering websites included the Open Directory Project, which was originally owned by Netscape and America Online before it was acquired by Verizon Media. This project relied on individuals who placed links to websites into an enormous hierarchical classification scheme. More than 90,000 people categorized more than 3.8 million sites, and the system competed with the formidable web giant Yahoo in the early days of the internet.[13]

The Open Directory Project is no longer active today, and collaborative filtering looks very different. That said, it is more common and probably more significant than ever. Users of social media websites like Reddit upvote and downvote posts within topic-focused online communities called subreddits. Through that process, subreddit users work together to identify the best posts on a topic at any given time. This basic model for generating a sense of quality and relevance—often mediated by some algorithm that aggregates the input of individual contributors—first appeared on early peer production sites like Slashdot. Collaborative filtering now plays a critical function in many of the most important parts of the web. It supports how social media sites like Instagram, X, Weibo, Facebook, TikTok, Snap, Google, and others identify relevant, trending, and influential material. To the extent that popular culture is now mediated through these collaborative filtering (and algorithmic) systems, an approach created through

Three decades after the model emerged, peer produced artifacts are everywhere.

peer production has suffused throughout the digital economy and society. These information goods and processing techniques may be harder to see than software or encyclopedia articles, but their impact is vast.

To sum up, three decades after the model emerged, peer produced artifacts are everywhere. Peer produced knowledge appears at the top of nearly every search result. Peer produced software plays a critical role in almost every stage of submitting and answering those search requests. Nearly every internet business model has been shaped by as well as draws from models developed and proven in the context of peer production. In this way and many others, peer production has changed how people produce and consume knowledge, from the most invisible elements of technical infrastructure to our user-facing pieces of content. It has changed the world.

4

CONDITIONS AND PROCESSES: WHY AND HOW DOES PEER PRODUCTION WORK?

Dana Lewis is a health communications professional who, like millions around the world, lives with type 1 diabetes. Type 1 diabetes is a chronic medical condition that impedes the pancreas from producing insulin, which keeps blood glucose levels within a healthy range. People with type 1 diabetes constantly monitor their blood glucose levels, and then pump or consume insulin as needed. The glucose monitors on the market when Dana was diagnosed, however, only issued alerts that were not loud. A heavy sleeper, Dana worried that she might miss an alert in the middle of the night and wind up in the emergency room. Prompted by a conversation on modifying her glucose monitor on Twitter in 2013, Lewis worked with Scott Leibrand to calibrate her monitor so that it could predict changes in her blood sugar hours in advance.[1] She shared hardware specifications and software for her solution online so that others could benefit, and began collaborating with a community called "Nightscout," created by parents of children with type 1 diabetes to build remote glucose monitors for their kids.[2]

Collaborating online with Nightscout members and others over several years, Lewis went on to coordinate the development of the "Do-It-Yourself Pancreas System" (#DIYPS) and an "open source artificial pancreas system" (#OpenAPS). These systems introduced FLOSS software and open hardware to act as a "closed loop" between a glucose monitor and insulin pump to do the job of a pancreas without needing any intervention by a person. More than 600 people used the #DIYPS/#OpenAPS system, and the system has been in use for over 1.3 million hours of safe operation. Through the collective effort of dozens of volunteers, the system has provided features several years ahead of any commercial products.[3]

Why were Lewis and the other #OpenAPS volunteers able to meet a widely known need that neither firms nor markets had been able to address? The answer lies in a variety of sociotechnical factors, which as the term implies, encompass both social and technical elements at the same time. In the case of #OpenAPS, these included a set of programming tools and work procedures that allowed people to join the community as well as implement the design of an artificial pancreas system in a distributed way without a boss, formal employment, and payments changing hands.

More generally, peer production projects like #DIYPS and #OpenAPS work for at least three kinds of reasons. First, peer production projects work because of their social and technological context. Second, they work through specific ways of organizing social groups. Third and finally, peer production works by harnessing the motivations of individual participants. These three types of explanations work at a *macro* level that corresponds to societies, technologies, and economies; a *meso* level that corresponds to organizations or groups; and a *micro* level that corresponds to individual participants. Each level emphasizes key features of how peer production functions. And all three levels contribute to realizing peer production's defining qualities of decentralization, nonmonetary incentives, and publicly accessible resources. Having pulled the strands apart, we then weave them back together to make a case for why only a few attempts at peer production create innovative, collaborative results while most do not. Many factors determine whether a particular peer production project attracts contributors, builds valuable resources, or achieves its participants' goals.

Sociotechnical Context

At the broadest level, peer production occurs because of a combination of social and technological conditions that arose in the late twentieth century. The diffusion of digitally networked personal computing made it possible for groups of people to communicate online and collaborate on projects like the GNU/Linux operating system. Institutions, movements, organizations, norms, and laws also played a crucial role in making peer production possible. For example, the free software movement and GPL supported the rise of peer production. Peer production also rests on widespread cultural norms, such as academic traditions around sharing information, data, and code without charge. Peer production emerged in research institutions like MIT, and likely would not have been possible in the absence of computer scientists' and engineers' social norms.

The presence of distributed collaboration technologies among communities with norms that supported sharing helps explain when and why peer production got started as well. Projects could take off when these social and technical conditions came together in an opportune way. Often the reasons why a specific project blossomed at a particular time and place among a particular group of people require deeper layers of explanation.

The growth of projects has a cumulative dimension too. As more examples of peer production have become prominent and the tools involved in their creation more widely available, new projects have learned and borrowed from the ecosystem of existing resources. Many peer production projects use the same technological infrastructure to facilitate collaboration. These tools frequently have emerged in innovative projects that achieve information sharing in new ways. Wiki software is a great case in point. The first wiki, called the "WikiWikiWeb," was created by Ward Cunningham to make it easier to collaboratively author web pages.[4] Until then, building web pages required the use of hypertext markup language, and pages could not be edited directly by a site visitor through a web browser. Cunningham, a software engineer, started building wiki software in 1994 so that he and other engineers could more quickly share solutions to common programming problems they encountered in their work. Wikis made it easier to publish and collaboratively edit these "design patterns," and the software that Cunningham created supplied a platform for a project he called the Portland Pattern Repository. Although limited in scope, the repository's "wiki model" of collaborative web editing inspired others. Two of these others were Wales and Sanger, the initiators of Wikipedia. Both Wales and Sanger lacked programming skills, so they reused software that was originally modeled after the Portland Pattern Repository's wiki codebase to support collaborative article writing in their nascent encyclopedia project.

Ushahidi, a mapping project from sub-Saharan Africa, provides a more recent example of a similar dynamic. In response to postelectoral violence in Kenya in 2007, a small group including Ory Okolloh, Erik Hersman, David

Kobia, and Daudi Were created a website called Ushahidi to help share information about violent incidents.[5] The tool accepted reports and verifications of events via email and SMS, and published them on an online map that would update with additional information. With these up-to-the-minute reports, residents of Nairobi were able to maintain awareness of the location of clashes between different political groups and navigate the city safely. The designers of Ushahidi quickly realized that they had built a distributed mapping tool with many potential applications. In the years that followed, they worked with organizations around the world to deploy Ushahidi to support other instances of "crisis mapping" such as the routing of emergency response personnel after earthquakes or identification of coastline areas affected by oil spills.

Both the Portland Pattern Repository and Ushahidi built novel sociotechnical layers on top of widely available infrastructure. With the repository, this consisted of an existing network of software developers who had easy access to computers and internet connections (no small feat in 1994!), an interest in sharing their programming patterns, and enough common understanding to write up the patterns, publish them using the WikiWikiWeb tool, and edit the published patterns. In the case of Ushahidi, the core developer group adapted existing mapping software and standard web-based authoring tools to support the collection, aggregation, and publication of information submitted by members of the public. Ushahidi capitalized on these individuals' shared interest in and awareness of the urban environment in Nairobi. The system also relied on the web and cell phones—technologies that were widely diffused throughout Kenyan society. For each instance, key pieces of communications infrastructure like personal computers, the web, mobile computing, and social media opened up new possibilities in terms of organized activity and collective problem-solving.

New habits connected to the diffusion of the internet and mobile devices are part of a broader trend toward "networked individualism" and a "network society." The terms refer to the many ways that core experiences of everyday life have shifted from place-based groups, like one's hometown or a local bowling team, to geographically distributed interest groups and networks of individuals connected by digital communications systems. Networked individualism is hardly an unqualified good. Some depict it as a tragic loss of a bygone golden age when people could count on their neighbors, associations, and other place-based community institutions to offer valuable social support. Others see opportunities in the transformation, and argue that networked communication enables novel forms of support, engagement, and cooperation. Both perspectives have evidence to back them up.

The shift toward distributed and digitally mediated social relations helps explain the emergence as well as impact of peer production. The creators and users of both the Portland Pattern Repository and Ushahidi relied on sociotechnical networks in ways that helped solve the concrete challenges of information sharing and collaboration. For the repository, WikiWikiWeb software made it much easier to collectively edit a single document on the web. This was years before Google Docs, Dropbox, Etherpad, or any of the other tools we use to do this today. The alternative at the time would have been a cumbersome system of submitting updates to one person editing a single document on a single computer. Analogously, for the residents of parts of Nairobi facing postelection violence, Ushahidi helped users gather, filter, and map conditions on the ground in real time. The prior systems for disseminating this type of time-sensitive geographic information would have been something like a phone bank combined with a radio broadcast. Ushahidi, by being more decentralized, up-to-date, and verifiable, was able to overcome many of the limitations of such an arrangement. Both WikiWikiWeb and Ushahidi proved to have broader applications beyond the initial needs they were created to meet.

The distributed and collaborative qualities of the two cases illustrate another key shift facilitated by the spread of digital communication networks and social media: Lightweight and large-scale forms of collaboration are easier today than they have ever been before. Consider the differences between contributing to a printed reference work like the *OED* as introduced in chapter 2 and a peer produced one like Wikipedia. To this day, people continue to send new definitions and examples of word usage to the *OED* offices. *OED* staff review these suggestions, and if they agree that one constitutes an improvement, they record the change in the corresponding part of the dictionary. The *OED* has only released two print editions: the first published between 1888 and 1928, and the second in 1989. At present, the *OED* website is updated with these changes four times a year.

In contrast, with Wikipedia, you can make a change to most articles directly from the comfort of your computer, tablet, or cell phone. You can change the live version of the encyclopedia immediately without creating an account, or getting permission from any expert or editor. Instead of waiting months or years for the next version to be published, your correction will be reflected as soon as you click the "submit" button. Compared with the *OED*, Wikipedia's system of information production and publishing uses widespread digital networking and computing infrastructure to provide incredibly fast, lightweight opportunities for distributed collaboration.

The comparison between Wikipedia and prior reference works shows how peer production projects rest on existing institutions in at least two other ways. First, when forming online collectives, people draw on earlier examples and schemata. Many people knew what an encyclopedia was long before Wikipedia existed. This common knowledge means that when would-be editors encounter Wikipedia, they understand the goals of the project and how they might contribute. The motto of Wikipedia—"the free encyclopedia anyone can edit"—plainly depicts Wikipedia as a familiar artifact created in a new, distributed, and freely accessible way.

In retrospect, the familiarity of Wikipedia may seem obvious, but when it began, there were already several other projects attempting to build free, collaboratively written, online reference works. When one of the authors of this book, Benjamin Mako Hill, studied these projects as part of his PhD dissertation, he learned that most of their founders believed the thing they aimed to create—a collaboratively written, easily updated document on the web comprised of many people's understanding of the world—was different from an encyclopedia (which they thought of as a stuffy old Enlightenment ideal of a comprehensive archive of knowledge).[6] Because these founders did not describe their projects as encyclopedias, would-be contributors struggled to understand the goals. The similarities between Wikipedia and the encyclopedias that came before it supplied a cognitive schema that helped people recognize what Wikipedia was trying to create, and how they might contribute to it, even though Wikipedia differs from the encyclopedias that came before it in important ways.

Clear templates and schemata help peer production projects attract new contributors.

Clear templates and schemata help peer production projects attract new contributors. If contributors cannot understand the aims or big ideas driving the effort, they are less likely to get involved. Over time, as the space of existing, understandable projects expands, these ideas can also expand to suggest new possibilities for new initiatives. Once Linux exists, it becomes much easier to imagine a project like the Portland Pattern Repository. Once the repository exists, it becomes much easier to imagine Wikipedia. Once Wikipedia exists, it becomes easier to imagine wikis on other kinds of topics as well as projects like OpenStreetMap.

Second, peer production projects draw on another existing institution: free and open access approaches to intellectual property that ensure the resources they build will remain accessible and reusable under permissive terms. As discussed in chapters 1 and 2, informal norms for sharing and reusing innovations predate the creation of the GNU GPL and Creative Commons licenses, but the existence of these licenses along with examples of large-scale, successful projects using them make it much easier for new efforts to follow suit. As with cognitive schemata, the existence of legal frameworks that support public information production and sharing streamlines the process of their adoption.

The accumulation of these technologies, social transformations, example projects, and legal instruments has made it much easier to start a new peer production project today than it was ten or twenty years ago. When present-day software developers want to start a new FLOSS project, they often use a popular version control system called "Git" to do so. Git was created by Torvalds in order to manage the massive collaborative development of the Linux kernel project. A company called GitHub (purchased by Microsoft in 2018) allows anyone to create an account and launch a new public Git project using a variety of default licensing options at no cost. GitHub hosts the projects on its servers, reducing the overhead of system maintenance and administration while allowing software developers to focus on writing code and building a community. With hundreds of millions of software repositories, GitHub has become an incredibly popular way to manage FLOSS projects. Although not all GitHub projects are free and open source, and most are not peer production, there are countless peer production projects currently in existence because platforms like GitHub have made the process of starting and managing them much simpler. Such simplicity is the culmination of a long process of contextual transformations and innovations.

Groups, Rules, and Norms

Even with all the necessary infrastructure and good examples, starting, growing, and sustaining a peer production project takes a lot of work. Pathbreaking communities like GNU/Linux and Wikipedia can make it easy to forget that most attempts to start a new peer production project go absolutely nowhere. Only a tiny fraction ever attract multiple contributors, and even fewer create resources worth using. A smaller proportion still—far less than 1 percent—grows into massive, distributed collaborations. Only a handful like Wikipedia and Linux have radically transformed how millions of people go about their daily lives.

What sets the exceptional projects apart from the rest? Organizational analysis offers a second level that helps explain some of this huge variation in success. We can think of peer production projects much in the way we might approach other organized groups pursuing shared goals: firms, nonprofits, advocacy organizations, or civic associations. From a practical point of view, all of these types of organizations need to recruit participants, establish norms and rules, coordinate and integrate collective effort, sustain collaboration, and generate valuable outputs. They can vary and be more or less effective along all of these dimensions.

Effective peer production projects—by which we mean projects that harness distributed collaboration to create and sustain some public information resource—overcome organizing challenges in a variety of ways. Because we cannot capture the full diversity of peer production, we focus on characteristic patterns. You can think of this in terms of sequential stages in the life cycle of a prototypical peer production project that sustains collaboration. All projects begin from an initial start-up stage, a small number advance into a growth stage, and an even smaller number become mature. At every stage, projects can decline or fall apart for distinct reasons. Throughout, both social and technical dimensions of initiatives contribute to their trajectory.

In the beginning, peer production projects start with the vision of at least one person interested in building an open, accessible knowledge resource. As we described in the previous section, the idea that gets a project going matters a lot. Clear, compelling ideas focused on understandable needs tend to do better than ones that are muddled or unfamiliar. In Hill's study of collaborative encyclopedia projects, only Wikipedia proposed to do a familiar thing (create an encyclopedia) in a new way (allow anyone to edit and access it). This combination—doing the established thing in a novel way—meant that anyone who showed up at Wikipedia in those early days had an intuition about the kinds of contributions that could help the project along, even if there weren't a lot of other instructions, examples, or rules to go by. This helped Wikipedia get off the ground fast and contributed to the decline of the other projects.

Good ideas will only get a project so far, though. Someone has to show up and do the work. Frequently, extraordinary efforts by one or a few people can help recruit other contributors to get a new peer production initiative off to a good start. Recall the case of the GNU/Linux operating system: Many people were skeptical that it was feasible for volunteers to create such a complicated piece of software before Torvalds sent his email announcing that he had made major progress on the hardest part of it. By doing so, a lone graduate student convinced a bunch of skilled bystanders to also invest time and effort in the project.

Social scientists call these kinds of early stage challenges "collective action problems." The term is general, and encompasses participation in social movements, voting, volunteering, charitable giving, and more. Crucially, all of these kinds of collective action can fall apart unless they reach a "critical mass" or tipping point of participation. For instance, in the context of peer production, a new project may need to attract some number of initial contributions or contributors in order to demonstrate that it is viable enough to grow. Many potential contributors will wait on the sidelines until they have some confidence that whatever effort they can bring to the table will not be wasted. Early stage contributions and contributors provide proof that the project has merit and legitimacy, thereby convincing others to join in.

Peer production can diverge from other forms of collective action because of the digital tools and open licenses involved. Someone can upload a picture of a sunset to a photo-sharing website like Flickr, say, and license it under a permissive Creative Commons license. Another Flickr user might come along a few months later and notice that it belongs in a collection of sunset images they are building and tag it accordingly. Years later, a third person may find the collection, discover and download the original photographer's work, and use it in a photomontage of thousands of photos of sunsets from around the world. These three people have, in effect, collaborated on the finished product, but this collaboration did not require direct coordination or being in the same place at the same time. The combination of a permissive license and digital platform enabled asynchronous, distributed collaboration.

The hypothetical Flickr example illustrates how networked communication can make participation in collective action radically easier than it used to be. In systems like Flickr, Wikipedia, or Ushahidi, individual participants can contribute a lot, a little, or somewhere in between. These discrete contributions can be organized and combined into larger entities that others can use or extend further. Benkler first described this as the tendency of peer production to work especially well for tasks that can be broken down into pieces that are "granular" and "modular."[7] Granularity refers to the size of the smallest possible contribution where a smaller size is more granular. Modularity captures the extent to which any individual contribution can stand on its own as an independent entity (the more independent, the more modular). In the Flickr example, both the original photo and tag adding the photo to the sunset collection are instances of granular and modular contributions because they stand alone and do not require complex integration. The photomontage takes advantage of this granularity and modularity of individually tagged photos to build a more complex artistic artifact.

Not all contributions to all peer production projects are so granular or modular. For instance, Wikipedia edits vary enormously along both dimensions. An editor might, in a single revision to Wikipedia, publish a new article about a newly discovered jellyfish that includes several thousand words of text along with dozens of references, links, and more. In a different edit, another person might add a missing comma to that article. Although both contributions reflect important improvements, the new jellyfish article is a lot of material and work (not granular), but is highly modular insofar as it can stand on its own and would be valuable to readers seeking an article on that specific cnidarian even in the absence of the rest of Wikipedia. In contrast, the comma is extremely granular, but its modularity is less clear. On the one hand, it only relies on one previous contribution to Wikipedia. On the other, it does not make sense absent the context of the article.

Most peer production projects share Wikipedia's ability to incorporate at least some types of contributions that are granular and modular. The combination makes it easier for people to contribute without dedicating immense time or effort. Modularity removes barriers to entry as well. You do not need knowledge of the entire encyclopedic project to improve any single article.

The opportunity for such variable contributions underscores another way that group dynamics work in peer production projects. Many kinds of groups perform better when everyone talks to everyone else and coordinates actively. Work led by Jeremy Foote has shown this is often not the case for peer production.[8] Peer production projects that coordinate by discussing the work being done are more likely to grow and sustain collaboration, but this coordination activity need not be distributed evenly. In other words, coordination seems to facilitate collaboration in peer production, but there is no advantage to including everyone in the conversation. As with heavy commitment and major contributions from early project participants, this indicates another way that unequal participation can help peer production projects get off the ground without relying on a massive group of contributors right away.

Participation in peer production projects tends to be incredibly unequal too. This highly concentrated allocation of work across people is what social scientists refer to as a "long-tail" distribution, which is commonplace in cultural markets and many online settings. The extent and persistence of inequality over time remains noteworthy in peer production. In successful peer production projects, an enormous number of people contribute a tiny amount, and a small number of "superstars" contribute more than everybody else—often the majority of work being done. This reflects a key organizational difference of peer production compared to more traditional organizations: Peer production projects can integrate people who want to contribute once or twice as well as those who want to devote a huge chunk of their lives to the initiative.

So far, we have concentrated on how the structure and patterns of group activity can help projects overcome the challenges of getting started. What about once things have gotten moving? If a peer production project manages to attract some participants and create even a moderately useful collective resource, the scope and character of the collaboration challenges shift. Communities that enter into a growth stage must find systems to manage participation, sustain collaboration, and respond to ongoing concerns like participant turnover, influxes of spam or low-quality contributions, and disagreements within the community.

To solve these challenges, communities formalize routines, norms, and structures in a process that social scientists call "institutionalization." Institutions are the written and unwritten rules that apply in a given context. Within a community, organization, or group, institutions encompass "the way things are done" and often acquire a taken for granted, commonsense character. Institutions can be formal, like laws or a chain of command, and informal, such as the unspoken norms that guide so many everyday interactions. Whenever someone talks about a community's culture, people's roles in that community, or the explicit and tacit rules that guide community members' conduct, they are speaking about institutions.

Institutions may seem unlikely or even contradictory in peer production, where there is often little in the way of visible bureaucratic hierarchy or formalized mechanisms of directing behavior. Yet precisely because of the absence of more formal structures and hierarchies, institutions matter immensely in peer production. All peer production projects that reach a growth stage witness, and seem to benefit from, the emergence and institutionalization of leaders, rules, and routines. Although these institutions may differ from what occurs in firms or other kinds of collectives, they are no less real and no less valuable for sustaining the work of the group. Leaders, rules, and routines (even informal ones) help participants figure out how to direct their efforts, ensure that ongoing projects meet agreed-on standards of quality, and help resolve disputes. Likewise, institutions can support mechanisms to monitor and enforce norms. This can range from more tacit approaches like peer pressure, downvoting, or negative feedback to more explicit ones such as punishments meted out by authority figures. As peer production projects grow, contributors and contributions benefit from some rules in order to preserve existing resources and support ongoing collaborations. In this sense, the institutionalization of a peer production project can signal that it has increased in maturity and stability.

Mature projects encounter new challenges as the tendency toward institutionalization comes into tension with the need to support ongoing growth and new participation. Once a project has been around for a few years, there might be a small group of highly dedicated "old-timers" who have shifted into mentoring or leadership roles. But these old-timers can become entrenched in positions of power and use their influence to prevent the ongoing evolution that sustains open communities. This dynamic plays out in most large wikis, for example, and famously in the English-language version of Wikipedia, where so few administrators are being added that there have been net decreases in active administrators in many recent years. Importantly, these processes are not simply cases of old-timers being malevolent or closing the door behind them. As peer production communities mature, they shift from growing the resources at the center of their efforts (e.g., encyclopedia articles) to maintaining the quality of these resources and their institutions. Communities need their norms to survive, and norms, like any other type of physical and social infrastructure, require maintenance and repairs to stay in good working order.

In a mature community, newcomers will be less familiar with the community's institutions than more established users. These newcomers may be less good at contributing in ways that established members view as high quality. Established members, even when their numbers dwindle, may find it difficult to accept and integrate newcomers or perceive them as anything other than a threat. In many cases, this presents communities with a difficult trade-off: They can involve more participants and sustain the growth of their projects, or protect their existing resources and institutions by continuing to rely on people who are already there. Sustaining a mature project requires navigating the tensions between these competing priorities.

Sometimes, for one reason or another, peer production projects die. In the ways we have described, people may simply stop showing up. There might be a big fight among some key community leaders, and a project may fracture into two or more subcommunities. An existing project might lose steam, and its remaining members may decide to merge with another group. In a best-case scenario like the GuttenPlag Wiki discussed in our introduction that was crowdsourcing instances of plagiarism by a famous German politician, a project may achieve its goals and disband because there is no more work to be done. Projects and their participants can have diverse goals, and for many, the cessation of the project may not be a problem.

Generalizing about peer production project death is difficult because death occurs for wildly different reasons. Moreover, little research has considered how projects end. In part, this is because the question of how projects worked in the first place was more puzzling. As peer production organizations have become more common and an understanding of their dynamics has grown, we hope that future work will devote more effort to questions of their demise. Among the largest and most prominent projects that millions of people rely on every single day, the possibility of project death looms as a terrible risk.

Participant Attributes, Motivations, and Actions

Ultimately, peer production projects only grow and survive because individual people use and contribute to them. Understanding how peer production works at this individual level is critical. Who are the people who make up peer production communities and what drives them to sustain commitment to difficult, often unpaid work? How and why do they create different kinds of peer produced resources? There is no simple answer to these questions. Many kinds of people participate in different projects in many ways for many reasons. At the same time, some important patterns characterize this individual level of participation.

Peer production contributors do not fit a single demographic profile or background. Some hold formal credentials or professional expertise relevant to a project, such as many GNU/Linux programmers. Others are amateurs and hobbyists who have no claim to expertise. Sometimes contributors to peer production projects like Wikipedia or Linux include precocious youths who might be barred from employment by labor laws. There are some peer production projects, like the Scratch online community where users work together to build and remix collaborative programming projects, in which the participants are almost exclusively children. Many projects include contributors from around the world and a wide range of backgrounds.

Contributors may be diverse, but they are far from representative of the world's population. While most projects make it possible for anyone to contribute, the people who actually do so tend to come from regions and backgrounds with more resources, better internet access, and higher levels of education and digital skills. Peer production is, generally, engaged in much more by the haves than the have-nots. These patterns of participation have multiple likely causes, including social inequalities and power relations. There is also evidence that peer production systematically excludes many people in both implicit and explicit ways.

The most widely discussed example of diversity in peer production projects' contributor bases comes from the English-language version of Wikipedia, where about 75 percent of the editors are male.[9] There is not a similar gender gap in readership. The gender gap among contributors has significant consequences for the culture of the Wikipedia community, qualities of the knowledge that is produced as well as shared, and downstream impacts of its content. By most estimates, gender inequality among participants in FLOSS projects is even higher than in English Wikipedia.[10] Beyond gender, recent research has documented gaps in peer production participation across education levels, age, rural/urban regions, language communities, levels of internet use skills and awareness, race, ethnic background, and more. In all of these cases, participation tends to be higher among people with more privilege, power, resources, and wealth. We consider the impacts of these participation gaps in chapter 5.

Why are participant groups not more diverse? Social inequalities matter, but other factors include how individuals choose whether or not to join a community as well as the pressures and norms that communities apply to the volunteers who show up. On the individual choice side of the story, preferences and identities can help explain who does what. Particular activities tend to attract some types of people and not others. This might be due to either the way people describe the activity or underlying patterns in society. For example, a site like Ushahidi will attract different people than those who contribute to the

Linux kernel or a genealogy project such as WeRelate.org. The kinds of people contributing to a site designed to help people navigate Nairobi are more likely to live in Nairobi. People interested in mapping family histories tend to be older and from communities like the Church of Jesus Christ of Latter-day Saints, which has a long tradition of genealogical research. The characteristics of the potential pool of contributors to each project will reflect those of the groups that are interested in each project's topic.

On the community pressure side, the institutions inside communities that we discussed earlier shape who, among the potential volunteers for any project, will stick around and become a regular contributor. In other words, communities tend to recruit and retain volunteers who fit into their existing culture. Because a core principle of Wikipedia is that content takes a "neutral point of view," this might mean that volunteers will be those willing to argue that their perspectives and contributions are neutral. Not everyone feels this desire equally, and some kinds of people—men, say—may feel this desire more strongly than others. Even a small initial difference in the distribution of these preferences would drive more men than women to volunteer and stick around. Over time, as the pattern compounds, the difference would accumulate. Wikipedia may have, in this sort of way, become a place where editors tend to be overwhelmingly male. Once such a pattern exists, it can be difficult to displace given that people start to treat it as a natural or immutable "fact" about how the community works. Underlying inequalities can be compounded even further through acts of harassment and discrimination. The combined result can be a participant pool that is far less inclusive than anyone hoped.

Among people who participate in peer production, motivations vary a lot. Global surveys of Wikipedia editors reveal some typical reasons. Some editors like the idea of sharing knowledge, while others want to fix errors or add information they think is missing. Some seek to build reputations among their fellow contributors, and others want to learn new skills. Some are driven by the conviction that the internet is better suited to collect encyclopedic knowledge than print media. Others believe in Wikipedia's philosophy of openness, free information, and collaboration. Still others wanted to make the world a better place. And some want to find ways to make money. The list goes on.

The reasons for participating in other projects vary widely too. In general, most motivations relate to advancing individual goals, contributing to an important collective project, or pursuing interpersonal relationships. Scholars have categorized some of these motivations along axes such as intrinsic versus extrinsic or selfish versus altruistic. While such classifications can help understand and predict patterns of behavior, none explain the full range of participant motives. Moreover, individual participants rarely report being motivated for a single reason alone. Motivation is complex and multifaceted even within a single person, and may vary depending on the context. The reasons somebody joins a project are frequently not the reasons they continue to be a part of it years later. For instance, someone might join to spread knowledge but stay due to friendships they develop with other contributors.

Individual motivation can be shaped by the environment in which a person works. An environment that emphasizes generosity and mutual goodwill may attract and elicit more generous and well-intentioned behavior. An environment that stresses incentives toward more selfish gains may elicit less generosity. The diversity of individual peer production participant motives is, in part, a product of the diversity of peer production projects and the different ways in which people can contribute to them.

As we have already alluded to, participation is also unequal within projects, among those people who manage to make some contribution to a community. Researchers sometimes talk about the "core" and "periphery" of a community. The core and periphery terminology relies on a metaphor of concentric circles expanding out from the most active, engaged participants at the center to the more casual visitors or consumers of the resources produced by a project at the edges. Within these nested rings, participants have different motivations and may adopt distinct social roles. Core members of a community often engage in more of the administrative and leadership work. Peripheral members might only make one-off contributions of smaller scope (e.g., fixing typos or reviewing content created by others). Over time, people may change their roles. A community may shift in terms of the distribution of participants, or participation across various roles and layers.

In many communities, new visitors start out by reading or consuming content along with observing the activities of others. In online communities, this is sometimes called "lurking." The term conjures an image of a creepy, silent bystander. It might also seem exploitative in that these observers are not contributing anything themselves. Still, just watching and consuming the work of a community project serves a critical function. And with many projects, it proves difficult to describe users of a resource as lurkers at all. Readers of Wikipedia, for instance, are not lurkers in the sense of passive observers. Rather, research has shown that by being around first without actively writing and editing, lurkers learn the basics of a community's culture and technologies. This makes it easier to become a contributor later on. In addition, by paying attention to the work of contributors, they provide an audience (or consumers) for the project. The presence of an audience motivates contributors, reinforcing their sense that the project matters and their voluntary efforts are not in vain. This means that lurkers or consumers are not simply free riding on the efforts of those who build peer produced resources.

Moving from lurking to more engaged contribution—shifting from the periphery toward the core—often entails a process of socialization whereby newcomers learn the norms and routines of a community, then integrate themselves into it. Although socialization happens in all kinds of organizations (e.g., through formal orientation programs or new employee handbooks), it involves unique challenges in peer production because of the voluntary and open-ended qualities of participation. In order to sustain an active contributor base, experienced community members must find ways to be welcoming and provide guidance to newcomers. Welcoming newcomers can also create opportunities to overcome some of the barriers to participation that we talked about earlier. Unfortunately, few things can deter an eager new volunteer more quickly than an old-timer burdening them with long lists of rules, guidelines, and requirements. A tension exists between welcoming new people with an appropriate level of formality and consistency versus making it as easy as possible for newbies to just get started however they see fit. As communities age and develop more established patterns as well as rules of participation, this tension grows.

Typically, a small portion of users or viewers to a project become contributors—frequently only a fraction of a percent. Among participants, a similar or even smaller proportion go on to become regular contributors, or advance from the periphery to the core. As we mentioned before, contributors often adopt specific social roles that may or may not correspond to formal responsibilities or authority. In a free software project, for example, some participants might focus primarily on contributing code for new functionality while others spend their time identifying and fixing bugs. Others might contribute exclusively by writing documentation or testing new software. The roles depend on a few things, such as the tasks involved in the project, technologies, and institutions that make contributing in particular ways possible, visible, or rewarded as well as the emergence of stable subcommunities or work groups.[11]

Among more active contributors, participants develop distinct motivations that sustain their commitment over longer periods of time. The most dedicated participants shift from instrumental or broad motives to those driven by community and social relationships. This makes sense since experienced and active contributors to a given project have, if nothing else, spent a lot of time working with each other. What may start as more casual working relationships evolve into deeper friendships supported by experiences of shared challenges and accomplishments.

Even the most active participants eventually decrease their activity or stop entirely. For many, these changes come about in response to moments of conflict or frustration. At other times, participants experience exhaustion or burnout following a burst of activity to accomplish a goal. In Wikipedia, there is a tradition of going on "wikibreaks" to disconnect from the project. In other cases, experienced Wikipedians who know all the rules will get so frustrated in an argument that they proceed to commit egregious violations of norms with full knowledge that they will be banned from the site for doing so. Alternatively, an individual's activity within a project may reach its logical conclusion. The postelectoral violence that Ushahidi contributors mapped so effectively came to an end, reducing the need to contribute. Ushahidi pivoted to supporting crisis mapping more generally, but the contributors frequently change from crisis to crisis. Likewise, the streets of a given city may be fully mapped in OpenStreetMap, and some of the volunteers may shift their interests or drift away from the project.

Bringing It All Together

As we have shown, many factors determine whether a new project achieves participant goals, builds valuable resources, and attracts contributors. At the macro level of context and environment, peer production succeeds because of the widespread diffusion of affordable, powerful computing resources, broadband internet access, social trends like networked individualism, and the growth of ecosystems around exemplary projects. In the case of

#OpenAPS, which we introduced at the beginning of this chapter, Lewis actively described the initiative online and others took up the chance to engage in the "WeAreNot-Waiting" community she started. The construction of the DIY artificial pancreas was made possible by the creative work of a mix of people with different technological, medical, and communication skills.

At the organizational or meso level, peer production works through a combination of leadership and design combined with effective systems to facilitate task allocation, content recommendation, and community culture and norms. The Nightscout open source diabetes community, for instance, is supported by extensive documentation of the technical setup, a shared platform for exchanging experiences and posting questions, and a tool set whose development is managed via GitHub. These organizational-level features of projects can change over time as a project grows, evolves, or enters into decline.

Finally, on the more individual or micro level, successful peer production harnesses diverse individual motivations and offers nonmonetary incentives in the absence of legal or bureaucratic controls. So while Lewis is the public face of #OpenAPS, it only prospered due to the many individuals willing to contribute to a nonprofit artificial pancreas system in an open and transparent way for a range of reasons. Individual contributions, roles, and commitments shift over time as well.

Our account here has separated the macro, meso, and micro levels of explanation for the sake of clarity. In practice, these strands are woven together and interact in complex ways. Individuals arrive at a specific project for a variety of reasons and gravitate toward a particular type of contribution activity. In doing so, they encounter, navigate, and may help construct or challenge that project's particular norms, rules, and interface design elements. They might begin to interact with other contributors, and over time, become more involved in community leadership activities. As this happens, a change in the external environment—such as the growth of a competing commercial platform that provides the same resources as the peer production project with newer, more intuitive interfaces—might change the contributors' experience or their motives. These changes could, in turn, alter the composition of the community over time or provoke shifts in the way the community manages its collective work. Those adjustments could feed back into the process by attracting different kinds of people to become new contributors or inspiring the community to overhaul elements of its technological infrastructure. Effective peer production, like other complex collective endeavors, depends on an interplay of processes at various levels.

5

CHALLENGES: HOW DOES PEER PRODUCTION FALL SHORT?

As some of the earliest and biggest peer production projects took off in the beginning of the 2000s, expectations soared. A radical new era of networked information production seemed to be underway. The success of peer production challenged orthodoxies of economics and management science. Peer production evangelists Raymond and Benkler, US writer and consultant Clay Shirky, and entrepreneur Rod Beckstrom proclaimed that peer production embodied a transformative type of decentralized, leaderless, democratic, nonhierarchical organizing. Arguments about the relative efficiency of peer production lay at the heart of these claims. In an era of affordable, networked computing, the old ways of creating and disseminating information through firms, market-based exchanges, and restrictive forms of intellectual property were being cast aside in favor of more open as well as effective models of distributed, nonproprietary cooperation. The rise of peer production communities had opened a window of opportunity through which we might leap into a more democratic, collaborative, and information-rich future.

Or so the story went. Today, more than twenty years after the earliest statements on the potential of peer production, we can see that these claims were overly optimistic. We can also see a host of other problems that few anticipated. Below, we describe examples of ways that peer production has fallen short of its advocates' expectations, reflect on why this has happened, and make suggestions about what might be done in response.

Getting New Projects Started

The high expectations that accompanied the initial growth of peer production overlooked several fundamental challenges of large-scale distributed collaboration. For instance, most attempts to create new peer production projects never get very far. Despite the highly visible growth and impact of a handful of initiatives, the experience of most peer production projects is much more modest. Most efforts struggle to recruit participants, attract contributions, or survive very long. The median number of contributors to a FLOSS software project, for example, is *one*—a single contributor.[1] The median number of contributors to a successful FLOSS project that has been released several times and built a contributor base is not much higher. In studies of peer production platforms that host many attempts at community building, most attempts at building a project attract at most a tiny amount of participants. Numerous FLOSS projects and most wikis are not host to peer production for the simple fact that there are few (if any!) peers.

This lack of growth may occur for many reasons. Projects are often half-baked as well as poorly conceived, communicated, and led. For sure, commercial start-ups and civic initiatives may also have trouble gaining ground. But the reasons and actions they can take differ. Peer production endeavors are usually not plagued by a lack of venture capital or institutional backing. They do not seek to increase their customer base but instead look for volunteer collaborators while at the same time trying to establish a form of organization (see our discussion of the importance of early contributors and contributions in chapter 4).

Entrenchment

Another way that peer production projects run into trouble also contradicts some of the early hype about "leaderless" and "nonhierarchical" organizations. As we mentioned earlier, the projects that take off tend to do so because of a committed and active core of participants, usually centered around a founder who acts as a benevolent dictator. When all goes well, the challenges and complexities that come with a growing volunteer project create the desire for more formal systems of governance. When this happens, project founders and early leaders tend to retain a lot of influence over the rules, how they get enforced, and how subsequent changes happen. That influence might be perfectly justified and legitimate, but it can lead to the entrenchment of particular perspectives or people, who can make it harder for projects to change or sustain themselves in the long run. This process has been described as "implicit feudalism" by University of Colorado professor Nathan Schneider.[2]

Consider the case of Michael Hart, a first-year undergraduate student at the University of Illinois at Urbana-Champaign (UIUC) in July 1971. On a particularly hot summer night, Hart stayed on campus in a materials science lab where some friends worked in order to enjoy the air-conditioning and avoid a sweaty walk home. Over the course of the evening, the friends gave Hart an account on the lab's mainframe computer, which was connected to the original Arpanet that would later become the internet. Hart realized that he could transcribe and use the network to distribute digital copies of out-of-copyright texts. He started with the US Declaration of Independence because he knew that all US government works are in the public domain. Within a couple of years, Hart and a small group of volunteers were working their way through various versions of the Bible and the collected works of William Shakespeare. They called their effort Project Gutenberg (PG), after Johannes Gutenberg, the innovator of movable type and the printing press.[3]

During the 1990s, PG took off alongside the internet and Mosaic web browser (developed at UIUC too), which contributed to the rise of the World Wide Web. A volunteer from Rome, Italy, Pietro di Miceli, built the first PG website in 1994. By the turn of the millennium, the project had digitized and released over two thousand titles. The growth of the web brought more demand for electronic books and volunteers interested in contributing to the project. One volunteer, Charles Franks, created a web-based tool to distribute the proofreading work involved in transcribing texts, launching a parallel community called Distributed Proofreaders in 2000. That same year, another volunteer and new assistant professor of library and information science at UIUC named Gregory Newby helped establish the PG Literary Archive Foundation to manage the financial and administrative aspects associated with PG. Within a few years, other PGs started to appear in Australia, Europe, Canada, and the Philippines. By the mid-2000s, these communities were transcribing dozens of books *every week*.

Throughout this period of extraordinary growth, Hart sought to minimize the organizational overhead and resist the bureaucratization of the community. He published FAQs and project descriptions that emphasized the community's openness, informality, and lack of rules and administrative procedure. At the same time, Hart and other PG community members took steps to manage an increasingly complicated, multilingual, transcontinental volunteer project. Some of these steps seem hard to square with the professed ideals guiding the project. For example, the same FAQ pages got longer over time, and incorporated increasingly specialized information about copyright, file formats, rules for becoming a new contributor, and the technical tools through which PG participants managed their contributions. In the early 2000s, Hart even attempted to spin off a parallel commercial project he alternately called PGII or PG2, which would have made the nonprofit and voluntary status of the original PG community much more difficult to sustain (the effort was eventually scrapped after pushback from some of the core volunteers).

Tragically, Hart died of a heart attack at his home in Urbana in 2011 at only sixty-four years old. PG continues, however, and in much the same form and spirit as before. The PG Wiki and other official resources still disclaim administrative overhead. The nonprofit PG Literary Archive Foundation continues to govern the project, and the number of guidelines, rules, and tutorials for newcomers on the site is bigger than ever. PG illustrates how the growth of a volunteer project can lead to more formalized and entrenched leadership practices over time, despite a charismatic project founder who espoused antihierarchical and antibureaucratic ideals. Entrenchment and formalization produce many similar effects across other projects, sometimes resulting in tensions and conflicts. English Wikipedia, say, has famously faced problems of old-timers "biting the newbies"—a term used to portray treating new editors poorly. These negative experiences tend to make new contributors feel unwelcome and lead to fewer community members sticking around over time.[4] The expansion of rules and internal procedures is also consistent with the growth and aging of other projects. Across multiple language editions of Wikipedia, the steady expansion of article pages has been accompanied by a parallel expansion in the number and length of policy pages governing contributions.

If you had arrived to edit the English-language Wikipedia in 2001 or uploaded a text to PG in 1994, you would have found yourself in a far different and less rule-bound place than someone who comes there today. Community leaders did not intend to make it increasingly difficult for new participants to navigate the thicket of policies and documentation as well as grumpy old-timers that now greet them on arrival. Rather, the challenges that come with running a massively successful and large volunteer project on the internet over multiple decades created administrative overhead as a side effect. As the content produced by a community grows, early contributors tend to develop a sense of ownership and territoriality too.

Furthermore, entrenched leadership can have darker, more pernicious origins. Between 2011 and 2020, a group of editors working on the Croatian-language edition of Wikipedia accumulated power and influence within that project, effectively capturing control of its governance.[5] These volunteer leaders shared radical nationalist and far-right views, and purged the community's governance system of anybody who disagreed. For nearly a decade, Croatian Wikipedia articles included Holocaust denialism and other misinformation. Editors trying to fix these issues were banned. Because the Wikipedia projects hold a strong norm of respecting the autonomy and self-governance of individual language editions, it required a consolidated, multiyear effort to unwind the governance capture of Croatian Wikipedia. This case highlights a fundamental vulnerability of projects that rely on self-governance.

Challenges with leadership and formalization in open or voluntary organizations are not new or unique to peer production. Community organizations, social movements, unions, cooperatives, and other kinds of groups have experienced them for a long time. While that may not solve the issues that communities like PG or Wikipedia face, the consistency of the pattern implies a path forward. In order to establish themselves, sustain collaboration, and survive, open, peer production communities must navigate tensions around the formalization as well as entrenchment of authority. Communities must strike a balance between the valuable rules and hierarchies that allow them to collaborate effectively, and those that no longer serve the aims or interests of the group.

The Least Efficient and Ugliest Way to Do Anything

The most difficult obstacles that peer production contributors run into can be each other. Virulent disagreements are commonplace in community projects and often constructive. Wikipedia articles on contentious topics improve when people with divergent perspectives contribute to them and hash out their disputes.[6] Not all disputes get resolved, though. Some result in horrible arguments, hurt feelings, and anger that lead people to abandon projects and communities they care about deeply. Communities can also attract vandals, trolls, or groups intent on doing various kinds of harm. Yet again, the realities of open collaboration turn out to be quite different from the stylized theories. Read through the archives of old email lists, discussion pages, or project plans of a few peer production communities and you might be confused by how much

The most difficult obstacles that peer production contributors run into can be each other.

time so-called collaborators spend arguing with as well as attacking each other, and trying to pull the project in opposite directions. How does anything ever get done?

Examples of different kinds of conflict within peer production communities abound. Wikipedia contributors engage in "edit wars" with each other on numerous subjects. What is the official language of Mexico? How tall is the fictional character Ken Masters from the *Street Fighter* video game series? Are mushrooms vegetarian? An early edit war over the name of a large port city—Gdańsk in Polish and Danzig in German—lasted years. Which name should come first? Should the answer vary in different language versions of Wikipedia? How? Should both names be listed in the first sentence of an article? In which order? Should they both be listed in bold type? Should it matter which empire ruled the city at the time of a historical event when that event is discussed? The debate became so heated that one of Wikipedia's most active editors was permanently banned.[7]

Because people in leadership positions are typically the founders of projects or those people who did the most work early on, peer production has struggled with conflict generated by leaders. Both Stallman and Torvalds have reputations for being conflict driven and argumentative. Some of the arguments had roots in disagreements over the direction of software features, project strategy, leadership decisions, and substantive concerns. But such debates have crossed into intimidation, trivialized perspectives, and emotional damage. The lines between substantive and interpersonal conflicts were blurry. Stallman's and Torvalds's behaviors provoked accusations of sexism, hate speech, and discrimination at the same time as they attracted apologists and defenders. Both men have now lost leadership positions in several of the projects and organizations they founded, in large part due to things they said and did to other people—especially women. While the disagreeable actions of both reflected their concern for and commitment to building better software, they also hurt their projects. The relatively low rates of participation by women and other marginalized people in projects led by these men—and others—can often be traced to such histories of bad behavior.

Another, related source of conflict comes along with the sort of porous boundaries and participatory design of peer production communities: spam, trolling, and vandalism. Let anyone contribute anything and it turns out that some unwelcome contributions will come along. Trolling or vandalism can be funny—at least to the trolls and vandals themselves, and sometimes to others as well. Nevertheless, with enough trolling or vandalism, communities can break down and the knowledge resources they created can become useless.

Consider Jeremy Renner's biography in English Wikipedia. In case you are not familiar with Renner, he is a US public figure known mainly for his acting work in films including several recent Marvel Universe superhero offerings and a couple of *Mission: Impossible* releases. His other occupations include singer-songwriter, musician, and according to multiple historical revisions of the Wikipedia article about him, velociraptor. How did Renner become a velociraptor, you ask? The origins are a bit murky, but apparently some anonymous memes gained traction on Reddit, or maybe 4chan, and resulted in a running joke that led somebody (or somebodies) to edit the Wikipedia article about Renner multiple times over several years (as recently as April 2020). You can visit the article about Renner, click the "view history" button near the top right corner of the page, and search for the most recent examples of the velociraptor edits yourself. You can also see how, each time the Renner-as-velociraptor meme rears its head on Wikipedia, some other editor comes along and reverts Renner's professional accomplishments back to a nonreptilian state. At the time of this writing, the Renner Wikipedia article was "protected," which means that only editors whose accounts have existed for specific amounts of time and have a track record of good edits can change it.

As far as we know, little harm has befallen Renner due to people on the internet calling him a Late Cretaceous theropod. The jokes come at a cost, however. First, they require volunteers to patrol, fix, and protect the page from vandalism. That time could be spent in other ways, either

How did Renner become a velociraptor, you ask?

expanding the encyclopedia or doing something else entirely. The jokes trade on Wikipedia's reputation as a reliable source of accurate information too. Trolling might provide entertainment, but it comes at the expense of a project's integrity. This is a sense in which the preservation of the quality of the content really matters. The more inaccurate things become—even things that seem obviously implausible—the less trustworthy Wikipedia appears. In addition, protecting the page involves a cost in the form of lost edits that might have been made had the article not been locked down against the threat of velociraptors.

In some ways, Renner's intermittent stints as a velociraptor are a best-case scenario. Disruption and incivility in online communities have far more grievous effects, such as discrimination, hate speech, threats of physical or emotional violence, abuse, or verbal assaults. Moderating the limits of acceptable interactions introduces vast, multidimensional costs in terms of time, effort, harm, emotional and relational work, and sociotechnical overhead. Volunteer moderators who embrace a certain amount of controversial or uncomfortable content can find themselves engaged in long-running battles to maintain community-managed standards, and that does not even touch on situations when law enforcement gets involved. Contributors to a project may act in ways consistent with local or national norms, but violate the standards or laws of other jurisdictions, including the community's own rules.

Responses often entail the creation or elaboration of rules and governance institutions, reinforcing the tendency toward formalization described earlier.

Perhaps some of the most complicated situations emerge when members of a subgroup or even entire community pursue shared goals that break the norms of ethical, acceptable, or legal behavior. This side of the internet can get truly ugly, and there are no easy solutions. For example, major social media platforms like Reddit, YouTube, and Facebook have had plenty of experience in recent years with militant, ultranationalist, and racist groups pursuing increased public visibility as well as attacking public institutions. Misinformation dissemination in response to the COVID-19 pandemic and vaccination efforts undermined public health in many regions of the world, leading to avoidable suffering, economic losses, and deaths. In some settings, peer production can become an instrument of antisocial destruction.

Peer production communities deploy various defenses against such threats to trust, safety, civility, truth, and health. Many defensive responses redraw the boundaries around what constitutes acceptable forms of speech and coordinated action. Some peer production communities, like Wikipedia, have long-standing norms of discourse that have proven robust to some of these challenges (e.g., the encyclopedic emphasis on "neutral" points of view, notability, and citations to reputable sources). Others like Reddit and other corporate social media platforms have struggled to define, monitor, and enforce consistent limits on user behavior. These challenges have sharpened as popular and political sentiments in many parts of the world have diverged on questions of appropriate regulation of digital public spheres in recent years.

We expect struggles over the limits of acceptable action and speech online to intensify. Of course, these contestations extend far beyond peer production and encompass the full range of networked public discourse. The challenges involved help illustrate an important point in this book: Open collaboration in autonomous communities entails social breakdowns in the form of disagreements, jokes, outright conflicts, and coordinated attacks. Some of these are entertaining or good-hearted, while others are mean-spirited, hateful, or dangerous. Some have parallels in other kinds of collaborative environments such as workplaces or civic groups, and others are specific to online collectives. Working together and sharing information in unbounded public forums can give rise to arguments, attract jerks, or lend visibility to fringe movements that threaten public values or health. Conflict can destroy communities as well as detract from social cohesion or the overall progress toward community goals and public goods. Other models of the production of information resources may involve different kinds of inefficiencies. For example, corporations may prevent some of these issues by imposing a private order of regulations on employees or contractors, but they also may not be able to produce resources of comparable scale or quality in some domains like encyclopedia writing.

Openness may bring benefits to peer production, but these benefits come at a cost. Projects must make difficult trade-offs between welcoming participation of all kinds and maintaining standards of quality, focus, and integrity. Inefficiencies and conflicts are the flip side of the same structural and cultural features that define peer production in the first place, allowing it to achieve all that it has.

Participation Gaps

Peer production communities are, in theory, open to participation by anyone. Yet the absence of formal boundaries hides the many types of exclusion that affect open projects. Openness gives systematic advantages to some participants and types of participation over others. The people who join and benefit from doing so tend to hold privileged access, knowledge, skills, or a strong cultural "fit" with the existing members of a project. Those who lack such resources are more likely to remain excluded either by choice or other, more pernicious types of bias and exclusion imposed on them. Many communities lack the resources to develop proactive initiatives that could overcome these

Openness may bring benefits to peer production, but these benefits come at a cost.

tendencies. Even those communities that do aspire to be more inclusive often struggle to make headway. As a result, many peer production communities—even some of the most inclusive and egalitarian in terms of their founding principles and objectives—are homogeneous in ways that reinforce social inequities.

Free and open hardware and design communities that apply peer production approaches to the creation as well as sharing of physical electronic devices provide an interesting example of these patterns. The hardware and designs are free in the sense that any plans, templates, codes, and specifications used to produce them are licensed under the same sorts of licenses first applied to FLOSS. The artifacts created through open hardware and design are frequently personal projects pursued by hobbyists looking to learn and play on a small, informal scale. Increasingly, though, open hardware devices have become popular among industrial researchers and product designers looking to create and share cheap, rapid prototypes. The domain of open hardware and design thus encompasses everything from massive, industrial-scale 3D printers, to personal electronics kits used in elementary schools around the world, to websites devoted to posting and sharing freely licensed computer-aided design files. The scale of these activities is enormous, accounting for billions of dollars of economic activity, numerous commercial and noncommercial innovations, and countless hours of fun and frustration.

One of the most famous and widely used hardware hacking systems is Arduino. Originally, Arduino referred to a freely licensed digital microcontroller on a small circuit board built at the Interaction Design Institute Ivrea in Italy in the early 2000s. The creators of Arduino, Massimo Banzi, David Cuartielles, Tom Igoe, Gianluca Martino, and David Mellis, made the first boards as research and teaching tools. Recognizing the potential, they worked to expand Arduino production and dissemination beyond their academic setting. Today, Arduino encompasses a vast ecosystem that includes the original boards and their descendants; a software and programming ecosystem that has grown up around the boards; various communities of people, schools, and companies using and sharing designs for projects involving the boards and software; and multiple for- and not-for-profit organizations around the world that support the ecosystems of the boards, software, and communities in various ways. The software is all free—"free as in freedom" and "free as in free beer"—and the hardware is licensed freely and priced cheaply. Most Arduino and derivative boards are available for less than US$50 and complete starter kits for less than US$100. All told, tens of millions of people have used Arduino.

From the beginning, Arduino aimed to make programming and tinkering with electronics more accessible as well as inclusive. At first, this meant reducing the costs and barriers for students and others to learn basic hardware hacking skills with the microcontroller boards developed in Ivrea. The open platform and ecosystem supported ancillary innovations that enabled it to spread into other domains quickly. For instance, in 2006, Leah Buechley was a PhD student in Boulder, Colorado, working on developing tools and materials to support the creation of "e-textiles" that integrated electronics into a variety of crafts, such as clothing and other wearable items. Buechley developed her own prototypes and templates incorporating microcontrollers and circuit boards onto felt and other flexible materials that could be sewn into circuits with conductive thread. She connected with a local electronics manufacturer who had recently started building and selling Arduino components, and eventually developed her prototypes into a new sort of flexible, sewable microcontroller board that she called the LilyPad Arduino.[8]

The LilyPad Arduino worked exactly like the other Arduino boards and could be programmed in the same ways, but it was round, an attractive shade of purple, and looked a bit like an electronic flower with small holes at the end of each "petal" that could accommodate conductive thread and be controlled as a separate circuit. Buechley used the LilyPad to create and teach people to use e-textiles, leading to the growth of a community of LilyPad users that deviated substantially from the original Arduino user communities. Whereas the existing Arduino user base was disproportionately made up of men and boys, LilyPad users were disproportionately women and girls.[9]

Gender inequalities sparked these inclusion efforts focused narrowly on gender-based inclusion. Early hardware hacking communities consisted overwhelmingly of men and boys even as they emphasized how building devices and code presented universal learning opportunities. The open communities and resources they created seemed to imagine learners who fulfilled the ideal of a "technologically precocious boy" that researcher Morgan Ames has identified as a common thread of hacker cultures and "constructivist" learning communities.[10] In response, some attempts to shift the technological and cultural focus of hardware hacking and making have increased the involvement of women, girls, and nonbinary people.

Although projects such as LilyPad Arduino offer a crucial pathway toward more inclusive hardware hacking and making communities, they are fundamentally inadequate to overcome the complex challenges of inequities rooted in intersectional social identities. In her book *Hacking Diversity*, Christina Dunbar-Hester presents numerous examples that illustrate a pattern across open technology communities: self-described diversity initiatives run up against the contradictions of rigid constructions of identity and power inequalities.[11] The predictable result is that "diversity work" manifests as innocuous attempts to increase the number of white, straight, cisgendered women from the Global North without challenging the underlying power dynamics that exclude people in the first place. Promoting diversity can, in this sense, undermine equity and inclusion.

Participation gaps along lines of gender, race, and other social identities pose multiple, overlapping challenges to peer production communities. At one level, these gaps and inequalities contradict the values of universal accessibility and inclusion espoused by many community founders and members. Such contradictions can generate productive tension as community members and leaders reflect on as well as push themselves to live up to their own ideals by cultivating more inclusive and equitable spaces for collaboration. The persistent inequities within communities, however, can mean that peer production communities (like other open technology initiatives) exacerbate social exclusion and disempowerment. Durable gaps and divides in participation can also contribute to biases or other shortcomings in the resources that communities produce.

Misaligned and Biased Production

The persistent participation gaps in peer production contribute to another kind of challenge that has to do with the products communities create. Peer production projects encourage volunteer participants to select the kinds of tasks they pursue and issues they work to solve. As a result, the solutions and tasks tend to reflect the priorities and interests of participants rather than any sort of master plan. We owe the richness and breadth of peer produced cultural resources to the fact that no company executive or agent makes decisions about which ideas would-be community members should focus on in order to maximize profits, audience, or a particular cultural vision. Yet the same flexibility and open-endedness allows communities to ignore priorities that almost everyone would agree are crucial as well as valuable. Important topics may happen to fall outside the field of expertise or interest of those actively contributing. Critical perspectives may remain absent from the production process, leading to outputs that fail to capture specific needs, voices, or points of view that would improve information quality. In other words, self-selection into participation and tasks makes it likely that peer production will result in goods whose qualities are biased in various ways.

We can think of bias in peer production in terms of supply and demand. One might hope that the highest-quality peer produced goods would be the most significant ones that people most need or want. In a well-functioning market, the existence of changing prices brings supply and demand into balance. In a peer production project where contributors are choosing their own tasks, supply may become misaligned with demand. Where peer produced resources supply critical infrastructure, unequal distributions of attention can cause bad outcomes. Take the Heartbleed bug, a highly publicized breakdown in OpenSSL. The bug rendered encrypted connections vulnerable to unwanted snooping by third parties, placing millions of people's sensitive personal data and financial transactions at risk. The ultimate cause for the failure seemed to be that a tiny group of overwhelmed volunteer programmers were maintaining a piece of digital infrastructure critical to the global economy. More people working on the project may well have averted the massive vulnerability. Computational social scientist Kaylea Champion has shown that such "underproduction" is widespread in FLOSS.[12]

In some cases, underproduced knowledge goods are caused by the types of participation gaps discussed earlier in this chapter. OpenStreetMap provides a helpful example because gaps often result in regions on a map that are literally emptier than others due to missing content and the absence of contributors with local knowledge. Computer scientist Jacob Thebault-Spieker and his collaborators have analyzed these issues under the rubric of a "rural/urban divide" in both OpenStreetMap and Wikipedia.[13] Thebault-Spieker and his colleagues have shown that peer produced content about cities and more populous regions throughout the United States receives more contributions than content about less populated rural areas on a per capita basis. The coverage of rural regions is of disproportionately lower quality as a result. With Wikipedia, participation gaps produce a wide array of content gaps. Authors usually start contributing to areas they are familiar with, meaning that those areas that eventually resonate most with the background and interests of the contributors receive the most attention. One consequence of this is that notable women are underrepresented on Wikipedia, and the existing articles lack credible citations and sources.

Social Media, Social Failures, and Social Correctives?

People frequently talk about "market failures" to describe, say, an industry dominated by a monopolist. Operating outside markets, we think about the challenges and shortcomings we've laid out as "social failures"—a term we borrow from sociologist Mikołaj Jan Piskorski. In general, these social failures are rooted in social interactions and relationships that pervade peer production, not because anyone intends them to happen.[14] Left to their own devices, large crowds of people collaborating on the internet can produce incredible, high-quality information resources. But nothing guarantees that these efforts will get off the ground, the communities will pursue their work in an egalitarian way, or the resources they create will reflect their creators' values and priorities. Even if the resources generated by peer production mirror the priorities of the people who produce them, inequality in participation may cause bias and further entrench privileged perspectives, at the expense of sustaining the full diversity and breadth of human experience and knowledge.

So whether in terms of start-up problems, the entrenchment of authority, or the costs of open collaboration, peer production projects frequently trip up on obstacles that other models of coordinated activity and information production sidestep by design. In this sense, peer production was never going to work as efficiently as the most optimistic observers thought. The largest and most successful projects have made some solutions to these issues look easy, but others (such as gender and underproduction gaps) have come back to haunt them.

What can peer production communities and leaders do in the face of challenges deriving from social failures? Extending the analogy between "social failures" and "market failures" further suggests some constructive guidance. Remedies for market failures, like monopolistic dominance of an industry, are familiar in economic theory and policy. Price-based allocation of goods may work well until, for example, some company controls the entire market for widgets, leaving it an opportunity to exploit the demand for widgets for its private gain at the expense of everyone else by suddenly tripling the price. Tools to prevent and remedy such adverse outcomes in markets include antitrust and consumer protection laws, taxation, and more. Effective governance and management of the social systems underpinning peer production may require analogous interventions to overcome social failures.

Of course, the devil is in the details when it comes to figuring out exactly how to pursue an agenda of "social correctives" in response to social failures. We find many instances in the landscape of peer production, including actions taken by nonprofit foundations involved in stewarding community projects and resources; private foundations, firms, and intergovernmental initiatives dedicated to sustaining digital infrastructure and public goods; or academic work to create basic science and resources to inform effective community governance efforts. Detailed discussions and assessments of these lie beyond the scope of this text, but we expect and hope they will mold the future of peer production in ways that avert some of the well-documented, widely recognized failure points we have described here.

6

OUTLOOK: WHITHER PEER PRODUCTION?

More than two decades after the term was coined, "peer production" has matured.[1] The mere existence of peer production was a surprise and puzzle to be explained in the 1990s and early 2000s. Today peer production is ubiquitous. Peer production is also much more well understood. Yet both the context and peer production itself have changed.

Taking a step back, it seems that two broad dynamics have emerged. The first is one of growth, maturity, and decline within the largest projects. The archetypal peer production projects—many featured in earlier chapters of this book—peaked along various dimensions more than a decade ago. The pattern has precipitated moments of crisis as well as opportunity and learning. The second dynamic concerns peer production initiatives in aggregate. New world-changing peer production projects are not being created at the rate they once were. Partly, this might be explained as techniques and approaches innovated in peer production efforts have been absorbed elsewhere. As a result, peer production now faces more competition and appropriation than ever, especially with the rise of generative AI and LLMs.

Growth is not everything. Neither the number of projects nor participants in them offer compelling measures of success or impact. Small projects may also be successful as project creators and contributors might achieve everything they ever wanted by having a place to record their ideas and leave them in public on the World Wide Web for others to find as well as use as they please. The fact that a handful of projects have become so big and collaborative is, in this light, all the more surprising. Nevertheless, such a huge pool of tiny and uncollaborative projects does not suggest that leaderless organizations are unstoppable.

The fate of peer production has been further complicated by the explosive growth and adoption of generative AI tools throughout the digital ecosystem. Most immediately, the widespread adoption of LLM-powered chatbots seems to undermine the sustainability and integrity of peer production projects. At the same time, LLMs and generative AI tools more broadly continue to depend on peer production communities as a source of training data and validation. This suggests that generative AI is not simply an existential threat to peer production, and implies the possibility of complementary growth in the future. Further, peer production provides models of collaboration between firms and communities to sustain complex information resources that may become useful as a variety of public and private actors seek to create alternatives to the products of a small number of dominant AI firms.

Where does all of this leave peer production? We suggest three perspectives on its future. The first is the most narrow, focusing historically on peer production's poster children of the late 1990s and early 2000s. From this point of view, peer production's days of explosive growth and innovation have passed; new initiatives in the mold of the old successes will likely be rare, and the existing projects will plod along or even decline. The second perspective revolves around the potential expansion of peer production into different communities and for different types of products. This orientation emphasizes growth through evolution. The third stresses peer production as a source of inspiration, and how new organizational forms, which are not peer production, are building on peer production's practices and innovations. This way of thinking underscores integration and assimilation. We anticipate that the future holds a mix of all three.

The Rise and Decline of Peer Production Projects

As the most visible and impactful example of peer production, we have leaned heavily on Wikipedia throughout this book. We will return to it a final time because Wikipedia provides us with several reasons to be concerned about peer production's future. Figure 2 shows the number of

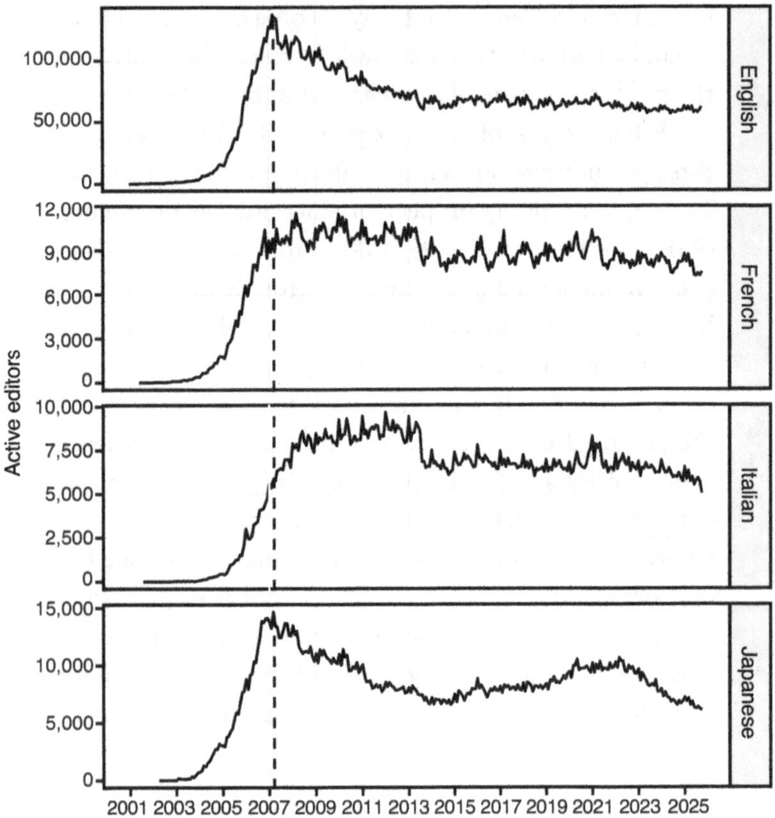

Figure 2 The number of active editors per month over time for the eight largest Wikipedia editions as measured by the total number of edits. Active editors are defined as accounts making at least five edits per month.

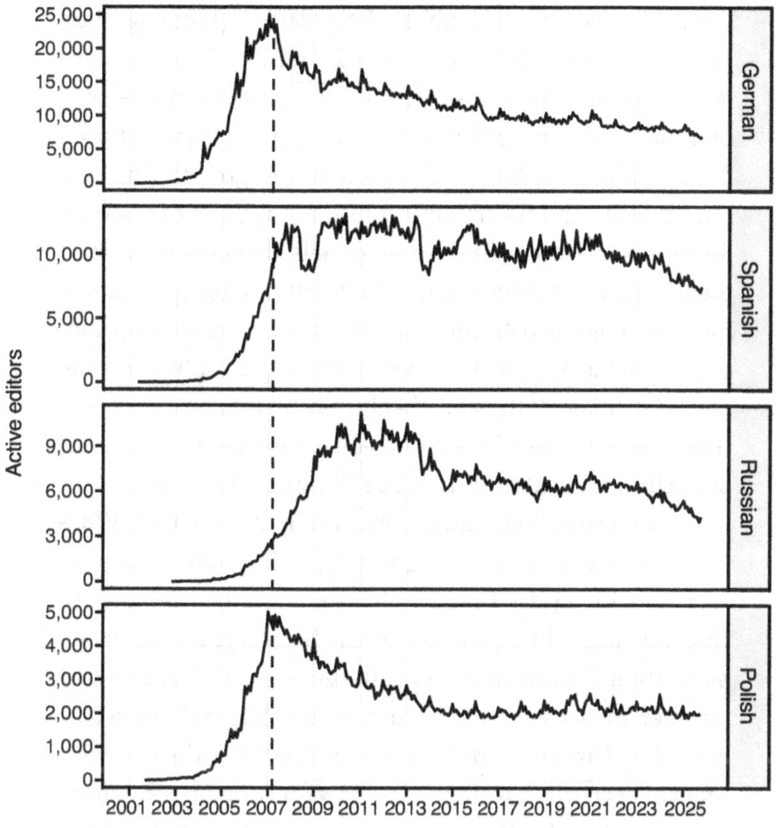

Figure 2 (continued)

active contributors to eight of the largest language versions of Wikipedia between 2002 and 2025. Active contribution here means an editor account that makes five or more revisions per month. The top left panel shows English Wikipedia's explosive contributor growth through March 2007 and its transition into a long, slow period of decline since then. The other panels depict similar patterns across the seven largest Wikipedia language versions measured by contributor base. In contrast, readership and other uses of Wikipedia have increased steadily over the period displayed. In both absolute terms and as a proportion of site visitors, Wikipedia editing has been in a phase of decline for well over a decade. What explains this?

The story of "rise and decline" is about more than Wikipedia. Many large and long-lasting peer production projects have life cycles that unfold over time in similar ways. This is evident in figure 3—drawn from a research paper by Nathan TeBlunthuis and colleagues—which shows the number of active contributors to the largest 740 wikis hosted by Fandom.com (formerly Wikia) over the first five years of each wiki's history.[2] To allow for comparison across communities of different sizes, the y-axis portrays mean number of active contributors in standard deviation units calculated within each community. The contributor bases of the large Fandom.com wikis follow a similar trajectory as the large Wikipedia language editions: an early period of growth, followed by a leveling off and subsequent decline.

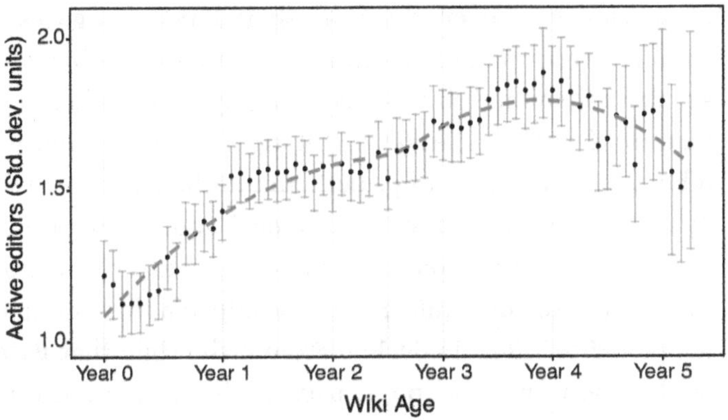

Figure 3 The number of active editors per month for the 740 largest wikis hosted by Fandom.com (the top 1 percent), as measured by the number of edits in April 2010 when full data on all wikis was available. The x-axis shows the age of each wiki since the first edit. The y-axis depicts the number of edits in standard deviation units computed within each wiki. Active editors are defined as accounts that make more than five edits per month.

Figures 2 and 3 illustrate a community life cycle dynamic that generalizes across a large population of wikis. The pattern also undermines two frequent explanations for English Wikipedia's declining contributor base. First, encyclopedic wikis with vastly different numbers of language speakers, and readers around the world all seem to have peaked after a few years. This implies that Wikipedia's rise and decline is not simply because the community has already written everything or exhausted the pool of potential contributors. Compared to English Wikipedia, the Spanish and Polish ones contain a fraction of the number of articles. Moreover, the Spanish Wikipedia engages a smaller proportion of the world's population of Spanish speakers than English Wikipedia engages the world's population of English speakers. Still, figure 2 shows they exhibit similar patterns of growth and decline. Second, the fact that the communities seem to peak at different points in time makes it unlikely that some single external factor can explain the dynamic. English Wikipedia, for example, happened to enter its decline around the time that Facebook grew in massive popularity or that Apple released the first version of the iPhone. But other communities, both Wikipedias and Fandom wikis, peaked at later dates. Beyond wikis, similar dynamics play out in other peer production contexts, including FLOSS projects and OpenStreetMap. Although it is hardly surprising that communities do not grow forever, the fact that they transition into decline—rather than simply leveling off—is unlike the traditional S-shaped diffusion curves that characterize many social media platforms. These rise and decline dynamics recur across diverse projects, languages, communities, cultures, times, and places.

If peer production communities have life cycles, what forces drive them? Can these tendencies be changed? What determines whether a community finds itself in a growth phase, or a period of decline or stabilization? A partial explanation derives from the reasons why peer production projects grow in the first place. As we have explained in earlier parts of this book, scholars and proponents of peer production have suggested that these projects grew because they were organized around deeply "open" institutions.[3] Peer production initiatives start off incredibly open from an institutional perspective because they have porous boundaries along with little in the way of formal rules, predetermined roles, or hierarchies—at least when compared to more traditional organizations. In ways that are less widely appreciated, this institutional openness may also be a function of projects' maturity.

Even today, almost anybody can join Wikipedia and pursue any kind of contribution they like with no more than a click of the edit button. This openness—the fluid boundaries and absence of predefined roles—made it simpler to join the projects and contribute than, say, to submit corrections to the *Encyclopædia Britannica*. Many other large peer production efforts began as similarly unstructured communities. By reducing the obstacles associated with collaborative production, such openness may have catalyzed the growth of peer production communities, leading to the initial phase of accelerating contributions in projects that managed to attract a critical mass of participants.

Over time, however, the initial openness shifts. Recent research—including some studies that we have conducted—suggests that the decline in contributors across Fandom.com wikis and Wikipedias has been driven by an increase in the rejection of contributions from newcomers.[4] In other words, the pool of potential contributors has not decreased, but the rate at which new contributors stick with the project and become regular participants has fallen. In this telling, Wikipedia and other peer production projects are declining because they have moved from an open model of collaboration to one that is more closed.

Why are peer production communities becoming more closed? Why would they cut off the contributions that sustain them? Usually, organizational closure emerges in reaction to threats that communities face. In English Wikipedia, these threats include surges in vandalism. Vandalism of Wikipedia articles can be innocent and goofy—like the Renner velociraptor incidents we discussed in chapter 5. But it can also take more troubling forms—like a vicious hoax in 2005 to edit journalist and statesman John Seigenthaler's biography to suggest that he had been implicated in the assassinations of US president John F. Kennedy and US attorney general Robert F. Kennedy in the 1960s.[5] Other types of edits may damage the reputation of the community and degrade the trustworthiness of the content it produces. For instance, North Face, an outdoor apparel brand, worked with advertising firm Leo Burnett Tailor Made to replace Wikipedia images of notable parks, waterfalls, and other outdoor sites in South America with pictures that prominently displayed the company's products and logo. This put photos of North Face gear on the top of the Google search results.[6] Multiple public relations firms offer services that involve surreptitiously scrubbing Wikipedia pages of true information that a client does not want to be mentioned in public.[7] Such attempts to introduce advertising, hoaxes, personal attacks, and misinformation into Wikipedia undermine the integrity of the encyclopedia in profound ways.

The threat of vandalism on Wikipedia has increased enormously over time. As the content, popularity, and visibility of the site have grown, the proportion of damaging edits to English Wikipedia increased from only 5 percent in 2004 to around 30 percent (between twenty to forty thousand damaging edits per day) in 2007 around the time that Wikipedia's active contributor base peaked. In this context, Wikipedia's increased rates of newcomer rejection over this same period are reactions to increases in both the amount and proportion of damaging material showing up on the site. The increase in vandalism provoked a defensive response, one aspect of which was the increasing rate of newcomer rejection.

Analogous rise and decline patterns appear in other large peer production projects. Early growth periods are followed by increases in attacks or low-quality contributions, which provoke the expansion of rules and enforcement practices, which in turn pose obstacles to newcomer contributions. Contributor bases decline as an indirect effect of quality monitoring and control activities. These are predictable challenges encountered by peer production organizations rather than peculiar pathologies of English Wikipedia. Although communities can respond to threats in ways that entail more or less collateral damage, many react with institutional closure to protect the resources they have built.

Life cycle dynamics of growth and decline, openness and closure, suggest a trade-off at the heart of Wikipedia's experience over the last twenty years. When Wikipedia was an obscure hobbyist encyclopedia project, there was little incentive to vandalize it and no reason to filter contributions of new content. Multinational companies like North Face had no desire to launch a surreptitious product placement campaign. Few people would have seen such images or cared. Wikipedia's growth, quality, audience, and impact created the incentives for vandals and firms like North Face, which now look to co-opt Wikipedia for their own benefit. Analogous issues have arisen for other large, impactful peer production communities, many of which find themselves victims of the unexpected consequences of their success. If they aim to sustain large pools of volunteers and a thriving community culture built around openness and accessible participation, they must find ways to erect defensive rules and practices that do not eliminate opportunities for continued growth.

The pattern is clear: Over the last twenty years, the biggest and most prominent peer production projects,

The pattern is clear: Over the last twenty years, the biggest and most prominent peer production projects have shifted away from exclusively focusing on building knowledge commons that are open to all.

including OpenStreetMap and several of the largest FLOSS communities, have shifted away from exclusively focusing on building knowledge commons that are open to all. The goal of participatory growth remains, but these communities balance it against other aims such as maintaining the quality of knowledge bases they have already created in the face of increasingly determined attacks. Where peer production could previously rely on policies of openness, the need to maintain quality means that projects have had to turn toward new policies of closure along with the formalization of boundaries, rules, and routines. The results are tensions and trade-offs as communities navigate the contradictions as well as conflicts that ensue.

The need to manage organizational boundaries and formalization may appear as existential threats to the ideals of openness and inclusion at the core of peer production. An alternative is to view these as navigational challenges that have emerged as organic and predictable by-products of some communities' success. Institutional closure in peer production is thus neither pathological nor a sign of failure. Instead, it indicates that projects are evolving and creating more robust governance mechanisms. Yet, adopting this perspective raises questions about the future of sustainable community leadership and governance in peer production. Given the centrality of peer produced digital infrastructure to important areas of contemporary society, we believe these questions are urgent, and should continue to be addressed through experiments, research, and design.

Inspired by Peer Production

In the final section of chapter 3, we explained how peer production's greatest impact may be in the way that it has inspired various other projects that share some, but not all, of the features of peer production. In this way, lessons from peer production have been taken up in many contexts. In some cases, this has involved splitting up and disaggregating elements of peer production in ways that seemed impossible.

Until 2009, much of online mass collaboration occurred in peer production communities. Alternatives were attempted, but they were rarely successful and typically paled in comparison to peer produced initiatives. GNU/Linux outcompeted more closed operating systems. Wikipedia outcompeted more closed encyclopedias. In fact, Wikipedia's two founders, Wales and Sanger, famously created Wikipedia to feed material into a more tightly vetted and expert-authored encyclopedia project called Nupedia. With a body of rules designed to ensure high-quality content reviewed by experts, Nupedia failed to attract more than two dozen articles before folding. Wikipedia succeeded because it was structured openly in ways that brought together the full peer production package.

Yet it turned out that peer production was not the only way to engage online communities in the collaborative creation of large-scale information goods. Experimentation led to new organizational forms and strategies that included commercial and venture-funded initiatives as well as more cooperative, autonomous communities. For example, a series of transgressive communities focused on sharing and remixing copyrighted content built on the peer production models. The website Genius (formerly known as Rap Genius and before that Rap Exegesis) allows people to upload, edit, and annotate song lyrics along with other kinds of content. The collaborative lyric sharing that helped establish and sustain the community in what was a legal gray zone (at best) under copyright laws, and has attracted multiple lawsuits from music publishers and artists. Genius, however, built on the informal norms around sampling and remixing that prevailed among artists and fans of hip-hop to grow an immense audience, attracting the participation of globally famous artists including Nas and RZA of the Wu-Tang Clan. With a large user base, Genius's founders attracted financial backing from prominent venture capitalists who were not willing to let some inconvenient lawsuits stand between them and the profit potential of the site's millions of visitors per month.

Genius exemplifies a hybrid commercial, participatory community premised on remixing content that confounds easy categorization. Even though it was founded as a for-profit venture, Genius exists somewhere at the margins of both peer production and the commercial web, analogous to the way commercial remixing sits at the edge of legally permissible content creation. The site has ambiguous encumbrances of proprietary licenses and contractual obligations, even if it only adheres to them imperfectly. Nevertheless, Genius embodies some of the key attributes of peer production, and relies on many of the social and technical design features that define it. The fact that Genius is commercial and not building a public knowledge commons underscores how the designs as well as norms of peer production have spawned new forms and creative output.

In another illustration, a vibrant movement around creating "makerspaces," "hackerspaces," or "hacklabs" has arisen, led by people steeped in peer production. There are thousands of making and hacking spaces in hundreds of cities and dozens of countries around the world. Such spaces draw on the ethos of cooperative production and FLOSS development. Often, they adopt nonhierarchical forms of governance and systems of peer-to-peer mutual aid that are directly inspired by participants' experiences in FLOSS communities. That said, these communities typically do not attempt to build a single thing together.

Many emphasize the acquisition, use, and maintenance of physical fabrication tools and computing resources that individual members can use to craft material goods. Such hackerspace communities are usually not engaged in peer production. Still, they have clearly learned from peer production in ways that allow them to flourish alongside commercial manufacturing.

The "platform cooperativism" movement offers another initiative inspired partly by peer production. The focus is on building cooperative alternatives and replacements for user-generated content sites, like Flickr, and gig economy firms, such as Uber or Airbnb. Unlike these platforms, which are owned by large venture-funded companies, platform cooperatives are managed as worker-owned, profit-sharing enterprises. Several early experiments in this area are underway, many of which invoke and attempt to build on examples of peer production. Fairbnb offers short-term hospitality services along similar lines to those on Airbnb, but through a collectively owned and operated model of organization that aspires to advance democratic transparency, accountability, and sustainability.[8] Another site, Stocksy, supplies stock photography and footage through an artist-owned cooperative model where licensing fees are distributed in a more egalitarian fashion, and with more opportunities for artist-members to participate in decision-making than with Getty Images.[9] Often these communities have clear boundaries—for instance, they might be oriented toward artists or drivers—and are focused on providing benefits to their members as opposed to the general public. In this sense and others, these communities are not cases of peer production. But they are learning and borrowing from the autonomous governance experiences of peer production communities.

Several scholars, organizers, and activists have also integrated ideas from peer production into other settings. For example, the cooperative economy refers to a well-established field of production made up of cooperative organizations like worker-owned or agricultural cooperatives. Perhaps the most famous illustration is the Mondragón Cooperative Corporation, a federation of worker cooperatives in the Basque Country that was founded in 1956, employs over eighty thousand workers across several industries, and is among the largest employers in Spain. Other cooperative organizations prevail in other sectors and regions around the world, including consumer electric cooperatives that serve many rural areas of the United States and the famous Amul dairy cooperative based in Gujarat, India. Recently, a series of governmental initiatives in Barcelona have sought to draw lessons from peer production and apply them to advance a cooperative knowledge economy. The idea, similar to the platform cooperatives, is to create internet-mediated systems that match people who need some service or goods with others who have one to share—all outside the traditional market economy.

Peer production has inspired governments and political movements too. Several Pirate Party organizations around the world (most notably in Europe) have incorporated support for FLOSS and free culture into their political platforms. In terms of their internal organization, Pirate Parties have attempted more participatory governance and crowdsourced ideation. The idea is to make the parties themselves responsive to their constituents in ways inspired by peer production communities' governance and organization. In one evocative case, a project in Iceland between 2010 and 2014 sought to partially crowdsource a new constitution for the country. A series of open public consultations and calls for feedback in person and online resulted in a draft constitution that was approved by a two-thirds majority of the Icelandic population in a national referendum before being shelved by the Icelandic Althing (Parliament). Other social movements—perhaps the global Occupy movement most famously—attributed aspects of their organizing practices to inspiration from Wikipedia, FLOSS development, and other online collectives.

Today, new distributed web technologies, services, and communities invoke peer production as inspiration while deviating from it in important ways. This includes decentralized social media like the Fediverse—a collection of systems including Mastodon and other Twitter-like microblogging services used by millions. All Fediverse communities ("servers") are operated independently. They communicate via a common protocol that allows members of one server to share messages with members of another, similar to the way that people with email addresses provided by different services and companies can communicate with each other. The result is a social media ecosystem without a singular (corporate) owner or point of control.

Perhaps most prominent, digital currencies like Bitcoin have employed decentralized blockchain and ledger technologies to build mediums of financial exchange beyond the direct control of state actors. Other applications of blockchains and ledgers include "smart contracts," such as those built on top of the Ethereum protocol, and distributed file storage and sharing protocols like Protocol Labs's InterPlanetary File System. Blockchain-based systems diverge from peer production in at least one key respect: Incentives for participation in the Bitcoin community and most others are extrinsic and exchangeable as money by design. The result is collectively governed currency and distributed file storage, both of which have properties of public goods, though they remain rivalrous and excludable. Yet, the ways that these communities leverage digital communication technologies, autonomous self-governance, and the mass aggregation of many small contributions draw directly from the peer production playbook.

Decline of the Peer Production Organizational Form?

The wider pattern of decline that may be affecting peer production is perhaps more concerning than the rise and decline of individual projects we described above. The larger ecosystem of the participatory internet has shifted away from the open communities that characterized early stage peer production and toward market-driven models. Many of these were inspired directly by peer production, but are closed in ways that allow firms to maintain control and extract value. Such market-driven models of collaboration may prevent new peer production efforts from emerging.

Just as community-based forms of collaborative production took off in projects like GNU/Linux and Wikipedia, experimentation led to new organizational forms for building and sustaining information goods in other ways. Chapter 3 ended with a brief discussion of Airbnb and how it had built the core of its enormous marketplace for housing along similar lines to a set of network hospitality communities that predated it. In particular, both Couchsurfing and Hospitality Club were online communities that predated Airbnb, connecting people who needed a place to stay with strangers who had an extra bedroom or couch. Both expressly prohibited monetary exchange.

Couchsurfing and Hospitality Club worked in part because they used techniques like peer-to-peer reputation systems based on interconnected networks of reviews and attestations. Such techniques originated in peer production communities. The creators of Airbnb adapted these tools to a venture-funded marketplace for "sharing" residential spaces. The communities built on nonmonetary sharing began to decline right around the same time that the use of Airbnb and the "sharing economy" took off. The commercial site incorporated more intuitive and appealing interfaces, customer support, mobile apps, and advertising that allowed it to grow faster as well as more extensively than its peer produced predecessors ever had (see figure 4). Critically—and the reason that the word "sharing" is in quotation marks above—Airbnb also built its system around monetary payments. Such payments and the venture funding that backed Airbnb may have facilitated the firm's capacity to overcome the constraints of peer produced predecessors (e.g., by paying staff to create those user-friendly interfaces and provide customer support). Airbnb is absolutely not peer production, but it seems unlikely that it could have existed without peer production to show it the way.

Apple's App Store provides another powerful example. When Apple launched the iPhone in 2007, users could not install applications. The system built by Apple to keep the iPhone clean of non-Apple software was referred to as a "jail" by early iPhone users. Because iPhone users wanted to write and run custom applications, a large portion of them—a minimum of 25 percent according to one analyst—

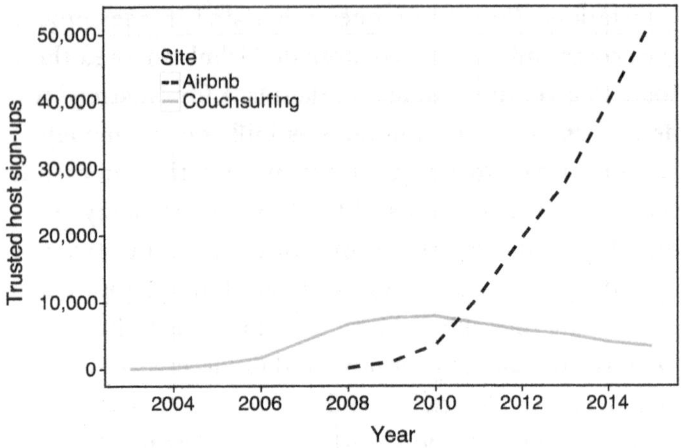

Figure 4 Number of trusted (verified) hosts on Airbnb and Couchsurfing between 2003 and 2015. This figure is reproduced from a 2017 paper by a team led by data scientist Max Klein. The number of Airbnb hosts eclipsed CouchSurfing at about the time that Couchsurfing plateaued and began adding new hosts at a decreased rate. *Source*: Author created, reproduced from Maximilian Klein, Jinhao Zhao, Jiajun Ni, Isaac Johnson, Benjamin Mako Hill, and Haiyi Zhu, "Quality Standards, Service Orientation, and Power in Airbnb and Couchsurfing," *Proceedings of the ACM on Human-Computer Interaction* (CSCW, 2017), article 58, https://doi.org/10.1145/3134693.

would "jailbreak" their phones to do so. Many of these applications were released under free licenses and developed in peer production communities. In response, Apple created the App Store, which ensures that anybody can create and disseminate apps in a decentralized way similar to what occurred with the peer produced software for jailbroken phones. In the App Store, however, Apple inserts itself in the middle of every transaction. The company sets policies and decides what software will and will not go into the store. Apple also takes a cut of any financial transactions between iPhone users and app developers. Sure, Apple's App Store software development ecosystem is "open" insofar as it extends software development beyond the boundaries of the firm, but it also allows the company to retain strict control. Management scholar Ethan Mollick has shown that many developers of peer produced FLOSS apps that had existed prior to the new arrangement removed their applications from the commons when the App Store created the ability to commercialize their work.[10]

The App Store and Airbnb's for-profit approach to "sharing" exemplify how firms have learned to enact strategic enclosure around critical parts of online communities producing valuable goods and services. These systems harness decentralized creativity, just like peer production communities do, but in a way that ensures that the companies retain control and the ability to extract revenue.

When the peer production model emerged, working openly in a knowledge commons was the only available technique for building massive, digital public knowledge repositories. Over time, large firms have found ways of harnessing open collaboration and community-based organization without placing the products of this collaboration in commons or decentralizing control among community members. The commons-based, decentralized model of peer production could, at least in theory, coexist alongside the sharing economy and private app stores. Yet beyond a certain point, the growth of firm-controlled, privately ordered models of distributed collaboration and information exchange comes at the expense of peer production.

If this pattern of competition affects the entire potential "industry" of community-based information production and exchange, peer production may eventually be replaced by something that is quite different in key dimensions. We find anecdotal support for a pattern like this. The emblematic peer production communities nearly all began before 2010. Linux was created in 1991, Apache in 1995, Wikipedia in 2001, OpenStreetMap in 2004, and Stack Exchange in 2009. Since then, no other peer production endeavor has attracted volunteers at the scale of these projects. Several of the largest, most impactful community-based collaboration systems, including Reddit (a publicly traded company as of 2024) and Github (currently owned by Microsoft), have embraced more aggressive revenue generation. The degree to which their products are available as commons has declined as well. They certainly have aspects and features of peer production, but they are different in crucial respects.

The shift of collaborative, community-based information production and exchange away from commons-based and noncommercial systems, toward private and commercialized ones, may or may not be a cause for concern. After

Beyond a certain point, the growth of firm-controlled, privately ordered models of distributed collaboration and information exchange comes at the expense of peer production.

all, mass collaboration and distributed knowledge sharing on the internet has hardly slowed down. What has changed is the way that it takes place. Whereas the earliest instances of peer production heralded the possibilities of collaboration outside formal markets and firms, more recent cases embrace hybrid approaches that blur the lines between venture-funded, corporate innovation and autonomous volunteerism. If GNU/Linux and Wikipedia were created today, we think that there's a good chance they would operate in a more market-driven manner with revenue streams and contractual commitments that provide direct returns to investors. Which is to say that they might not be peer production at all.

Peer Production and AI

The rise of generative AI and LLMs presents another major transformation that implicates the future of peer production. Earlier, in chapter 3, we introduced some of the ways that generative AI and LLMs rely heavily on peer production projects as valuable sources of training data. Ironically, the existence of generative AI may also threaten the survival of the peer produced goods it depends on. Consider the social Q&A platform Stack Exchange and its most popular community, Stack Overflow, which supplies peer-to-peer programming support. The release of OpenAI's

ChatGPT—designed as a chatbot interface to query an underlying LLM—appears to have caused substantial decreases in new contributions to StackOverflow.[11] Because ChatGPT has been trained on StackOverflow data, users find little need to visit the original source. And given that these users are asking questions to ChatGPT instead of on public platforms, updated databases of answers never enter the commons. Even the questions people ask remain enclosed in OpenAI's private databases.

The fact that AIs are bootstrapped from and continue to depend deeply on peer produced knowledge bases creates an underlying tension. If ChatGPT and similar systems drive down contributions to peer production communities, they will lose critical sources of training data in the form of trustworthy content created and reviewed by humans on which to build as well as refine future versions of their models. Training AI models on synthetic, AI-generated data leads performance to decline rapidly in a process known as "model collapse." If the AI ecosystem and investors behind it destroy peer production, they will have created a resource scarcity problem that threatens their own viability. AI tools also provide opportunities to supercharge attacks from spammers, vandals, and hackers, and influence operations interested in undermining the integrity of peer produced knowledge commons. Because generative AI allows computers to act in ways that are so humanlike, bad actors using AI tools can evade spam and bot detection systems designed to prevent this behavior. Such potential abuses expand the risks to which peer production communities are already exposed and may overtax their capacity to respond effectively.

In contrast to these concerns, generative AI may lead to the creation of new tools to support and sustain peer production communities. For instance, many of the challenges facing Wikipedia editors in underresourced languages—quality translation, automated error detection and correction, and monitoring incoming contributions for signs of vandalism or spam—can all be addressed through AI-supported systems. One of peer productions' more exciting recent successes is the Wikidata project, introduced in chapter 3. One reason that Wikidata is so successful is that its structured content means that it can be produced by relatively small groups of peers whose work is leveraged by bots, many of which are powered by AI. Today, the large majority of contributions to Wikidata are completed by bots, not humans. In this sense, the nature of Wikidata work means that bots act as a sort of force multiplier for a relatively small group of peers.

There are intriguing opportunities related to the peer production of AI models themselves too. A peer produced AI might be free to use, share, and modify in ways that mean that AI better serves the broad needs of global societies rather than only the small number of massive companies that presently control access to these systems. Indeed, some of the most advanced AI models are being developed in ways that are open, collaboratively produced, and freely licensed in some respects. The creators of these "open" models, including companies like Meta, cite peer production as justification for their permissiveness and transparency. That said, the production of these models still involves enormous capital investments to support massive server farms and a rapacious appetite for data. They also draw on copyrighted content from the web for model training purposes. These data are increasingly only available with permission and cannot become part of a commons.

Will capable peer produced AI models emerge in the future? Will people simply stop contributing content to peer produced knowledge resources when chatbots and agents powered by generative AIs can provide plausible answers to their questions or help them find high-quality information? Will AI-powered bots and agents overwhelm the capacity of community volunteers to maintain resource quality and fend off spam? Or will AI-powered community support tools enable peer production projects to expand and survive in the face of these new threats? Only time will tell.

Three Perspectives on the Future of Peer Production

So where does this leave peer production? We offer three points of view on peer production's future. The first is the most pessimistic: Peer production is a turn-of-the-millennium dinosaur, and this book will become its epitaph. Legal scholar Tim Wu has described information and communication technology industries through cycles of innovation, fragmentation, and consolidation, in which old modes of production and incumbent firms are replaced by upstart outsiders, who then struggle until a small number of dominant players exert monopolistic control.[12] In this sense, peer production is best understood as an outdated relic: a driver of innovation and fragmentation in a previous cycle, and soon-to-be loser in the ensuing wave of consolidation.

Evidence for this perspective is real. High-impact peer production initiatives are simply not being founded at the rate that they once were. In some cases, markets are competing directly with peer services and supplanting peer production. For example, in a study of Google Maps expansion by economists Abhishek Nagaraj and Henning Piezunka, the authors show that Google's launch of a system that allowed users to contribute to its proprietary maps led to a massive (about 55 percent) decrease in contributions to the peer produced OpenStreetMap project.[13]

That said, evidence of direct competition is still rare. Even a comparable commercial service such as Airbnb diverges from voluntary exchanges like Couchsurfing in ways that would be impossible to replicate within a "pure" peer production model. In this sense, Airbnb is creating vast new demand for digitally networked hospitality services that Couchsurfing never would have. If peer production is collapsing, it may be due to market-oriented entities learning to harness distributed collaboration in ways that neither older firms nor older peer production communities could.

The second perspective points to a continued role for peer production, but in a new set of shifting contexts. In this view, only the first generation of peer production should be characterized as the domain of hobbyists and amateurs. A new generation of peer production may be driven by collaboration between distinct types of peers—companies, industries, cooperatives, governments, and so on—working in distinct arenas. Future directions for growth, then, may lie far from past successes and require a large step back to recognize.

Support for this outlook comes from observing where and how FLOSS has flourished over the last few decades. Strikingly, the peers active in many of the more recent FLOSS successes are giant firms. Android, for instance, was created in 2008 and has perhaps the largest install base of any FLOSS project beyond Linux. Although Android's code is released as a commons, labor is almost exclusively paid for by large companies that benefit from Android by making and selling phones. Control of the codebase is theoretically open and anybody can download a copy of the Android Open Source Project. In practice, participation and control are highly centralized. Anyone may be able to download the Android source code, but it's only useful if you have the capital necessary to build a phone. If someone finds a bug in their Android phone, they likely cannot upload a fix because changing one's phone operating system requires special technology and skills and because many phones are locked down so that only manufacturers or carriers can update the software running on end users' devices.

Google owns the key assets to Android and employs most of the core developers. The free license on Android means that Google is able to bring together engineering efforts with people at Samsung, LG, OnePlus, and other large-scale producers of cell phones. These companies are engaged in something that might be understood as peer production, although the motivations and players are so different that it is almost unrecognizable. The only people who enjoy the four freedoms of running, copying, distributing, and altering the code on the mobile operating system are the large companies that make and sell phones. Similar situations prevail across embedded systems built on FLOSS. It's still peer production, but the people and entities being engaged and empowered in the process are very different from the earlier days.

Cloud computing technology offers a similar story of FLOSS tools supporting carry-on innovations in industries concentrated among firms. For example, HADOOP is a system originally produced by Yahoo that became the basis of multiple map-reduce products from other companies. Google launched the TensorFlow system, which supports many AI applications. OpenStack, produced by a group of companies including IBM, its subsidiary Red Hat, and HP, forms the backbone of many cloud offerings that are installed by major companies. OpenStack is FLOSS, but its users are typically large companies. As with Android, OpenStack is designed to empower the companies developing and deploying cloud services. In this sense, some of the liberatory potential of peer production—or at least free software and free culture—seems to be diluted.

The third and final perspective on the future shifts to the ways that peer production supplies continuing inspiration. At a basic level, firms have learned from peer production. The concept of "innersourcing," for example, describes a model of software development that involves large companies organizing their internal software development processes like FLOSS projects using similar collaboration technologies and practices. Innersourcing is not peer production, but it can bring quite a few of the benefits of it to far less open contexts. In addition, online communities and platforms have adopted features from peer production to become engines of innovation and growth in cultural industries. Content remixing, collaborative systems of filtering and ranking, and community-based models of moderation as well as governance prevail across large swaths of the commercial, enclosed internet. Peer production's approach, it turns out, was more transferable than many thought.

Instances like these suggest that peer production's most long-lasting impacts may be through the adoption of distributed collaboration techniques and organizational practices. Yet we anticipate that peer production can also inspire and support broader social transformations and impacts. The last few chapters of Benkler's book *The Wealth of Networks* raise this possibility, and the jury remains out. Could peer production drive broader economic transformations? The government of the Indian state of Kerala has made deep investments in FLOSS as a way of pursuing a place for itself in the global software industry, and in line with ideological commitments to free knowledge and commons. Brazil has made similar investments in FLOSS and free cultural works in the past. Governments in Berlin, Barcelona, and the Catalan region have taken similar steps. Many of these political entities have pursued peer production as a means toward technological and economic autonomy as well as expressions of egalitarian, collectivist values. The ideological elements of peer production may cast a long shadow into the future as societies continue to integrate new technologies and modes of production. While these administrative efforts stress the indispensable place that peer production now possesses, its future may lie outside of them too. Just as peer production has given birth to many unexpected projects, it has the potential to surprise us again and again.

Conclusion

We anticipate that the future of peer production will incorporate elements of all three of the perspectives outlined above. The halcyon days of "classic" examples of peer production are likely behind us, even as we will continue to witness the expansion of peer produced resources and models integrated into core social and economic activities. Past, present, and future instances of peer production will continue to inspire adaptations of similar organizing strategies and technologies in novel domains that we cannot yet anticipate.

It may be instructive to consider some features of peer production's past in this regard. The early successes of peer production often occurred in domains where firms and other incumbents had either not figured out how to solve tough problems, where existing solutions left unmet demands on the table, or nobody was willing to invest resources in a project deemed to be high risk with a low likelihood of success. In other words, peer production thrived at the margins or interstices of existing activities in the information economy. Partly due to peer productions' own impact, the areas we

Past, present, and future instances of peer production will continue to inspire adaptations of similar organizing strategies and technologies in novel domains that we cannot yet anticipate.

think of when we talk about successful cases of peer production are no longer marginal or interstitial at all.

The most promising arenas for peer production in the future may lie at the edges of its current domains. Perhaps these include blockchain-based experiments in social accountability and transactions, self-hacking, and platforms experimenting with alternative models of governance and ownership. They almost certainly include arenas we have not considered. There are always spaces where a few committed people can come together to try something different, build something new together, and share the products of their joint effort freely with the rest of the world. While many such future efforts will not be peer production, they will borrow from the peer production toolbox and build on its achievements.

We could conclude the book on an elegiac note, focusing exclusively on the gloom-and-doom side of our story. The most storied peer production communities appear past their peaks. Some of the most innovative, public-spirited, and transformative parts of the web that helped build invaluable digital infrastructure relied on by billions today cannot compete with venture-funded and for-profit alternatives that have found ways to enclose as well as extract resources that might have been shared more widely. These are fair, accurate interpretations that make us concerned about our collective ability to build a world in which everyone enjoys free access to the sum of all knowledge in the future.

Still other stories may emerge. Thinking about life cycles over peer productions' first decades opens up several strategic opportunities. First, a deeper understanding of the patterns of community development that impact peer production initiatives can inform policy interventions aimed at sustaining both the resources that peer production has created and communities of volunteers that have built them. Second, and in an analogous way, thinking about the past and present trajectories of peer production communities more broadly can justify opportunistic investments in the peer produced resources that currently exist as well as those that might be created. Open access, peer produced knowledge bases have enabled follow-on innovations, wealth, and social benefits that peer production's early participants never saw coming. Technologists, policymakers, and communities can intentionally orient collective investment and incentives to produce shared resources that distribute similar social benefits even more broadly in the future.

Although the conditions that allowed digital knowledge commons to emerge and grow have shifted, peer production continues to shape the world. Sustaining the value that has been created by peer production will require different resources and tactics going forward. Much remains to be learned from peer production to create new opportunities as well. These are the challenges that lie ahead.

ACKNOWLEDGMENTS

In addition to coining the term that serves as both the title and subject of the book, Yochai Benkler has been a source of inspiration as well as intellectual and personal support for all of us throughout our careers. Work on the early stages of the manuscript was assisted by Siying Luo at Northwestern University. The Center for Advanced Study in the Behavioral Sciences at Stanford University, Margaret Levi, and the center's Fellows classes of 2017 and 2018 also provided support, inspiration, and a wonderful context in which to develop many of these ideas. Gita Devi Manaktala, Janice Audet, and Suraiya Jetha at the MIT Press have supplied invaluable support for and patience with this project from start to finish. We also thank Deborah Cantor-Adams and Cindy Milstein whose careful editing improved the manuscript enormously. Mako and Aaron benefited from feedback and support from members of their research group, the Community Data Science Collective, in numerous ways that have shaped this manuscript too.

Of course, the most important group to acknowledge is the volunteer contributors to FLOSS, Wikipedia, and every other peer production project. Thank you all for dedicating your time and energy—whether a few seconds or few decades of your lives—to sharing your work and enriching the commons. Because contributors to peer production have been so generous in making the products of their work freely available, it was crucial to us that the text of this book be freely available and part of the commons as well. The financial support needed to realize this goal was provided by the Centre for Media, Communication and Information seed funding, the University of Bremen, Chemnitz University of Technology, and the Northwestern University Library's Open Access Fund. Other financial support was provided by the US National Science Foundation (awards IIS-1617129, IIS-1617468, IIS-1910202, and IIS-2045055).

Last but not least, we would like to dedicate this book to our families, without whom absolutely none of this would have happened.

GLOSSARY

Common-property regimes (CPR)
Common-property regimes manage the allocation and usage of commons goods.

Commons or **commons goods**
Commons or commons goods are cultural or natural resources that are held jointly in common.

Copyleft
Copyleft is a legal provision that grants the rights to use, modify, share, and copy a work with the requirement to preserve the same rights in all derivatives.

Copyright
Copyright is a legal principle that gives creators of content expressed in some medium an exclusive privilege to determine acceptable uses of their work for a specified period of time.

Creative Commons
Creative Commons is a US nonprofit that has released a number of copyright licenses that enable content creators to reserve or waive rights of using as well as appropriating creative works.

Firm
A firm is a form of organizing cooperation based on work contracts, division of labor, and hierarchy.

FLOSS
A common acronym that stands for "Free/Libre Open Source Software." Refer to the definitions for "free software" and "open source" in this glossary. Although we do not use it, the acronym FOSS is also common.

Free Software
Free software is software that is distributed under terms that allow users to use, modify, share, and copy it along with any adapted version.

Geek
Geek is an enthusiast with a strong focus on a small area of knowledge or expertise, often in technology or fandom.

GNU
GNU is a computer operating system, and one of the main examples and innovative projects of free software. The name is a recursive acronym that stands for "GNU Is Not Unix."

Hacker
A hacker is a computer expert who solves problems in creative ways, frequently by nonstandard methods or using tools beyond their anticipated purpose.

Hardware
Hardware encompasses the physical elements of computers and telecommunications systems.

Intellectual Property
Intellectual property is the legally codified rights of ownership and control over the access, dissemination, and use of knowledge goods conferred on the creators of various kinds of works. This includes multiple legal instruments such as copyright, patents, and trademarks.

Kernel
The kernel is the core component of a computer operating system that manages communication between the software and hardware.

License
A license is a legal permission, often used to define (un)acceptable uses of intellectual property.

Linux
Linux is an open source computer operating system created through collaboration. It is also known as GNU/Linux. See "GNU."

Market
Market is a form of organizing cooperation and exchange through prices.

Mozilla
Mozilla is a free software community and nonprofit organization responsible, among other things, for the Firefox web browser and Thunderbird email client.

Netscape
Netscape was a computer service company best known for its Netscape web browser before it was acquired by AOL in 1999.

Online community
An online community is a group of people coming together via digitally networked telecommunications systems involving the internet.

Open Source
Open source is computer source code made available for reuse, modification, and distribution.

OpenStreetMap
OpenStreetMap is a large online community creating a detailed digital map of the world through peer production.

Ownership
Ownership is the legal possession of a good.

Peer
Peer usually refers to someone equal to someone else in some kind of capacity like age or social class. In computer systems, the term refers to interconnected functional units.

Private goods
Private goods are owned by someone holding exclusive rights to that good.

Property
Property is a system of rights over goods predicated on ownership and exclusion.

Public domain
The public domain is made up of all the creative works that do not fall under exclusive property rights.

Public goods
Public goods cannot be (easily) used up and are difficult to confine. Examples include clean air, legitimate government, and public lands.

Sharing economy
The sharing economy is a domain of exchange predicated on owners of goods making excess capacity available to others. While the idea of "sharing" implies the absence of money, a group of firms operating for-profit online platforms such as Airbnb and Uber have attached different connotations to the term in recent years.

Software
Software is all the nonphysical elements of computers and telecommunications systems.

Transaction costs
Transaction costs include any costs involved in completing an economic exchange. Such costs may be monetary, legal, or bureaucratic, and accrue in the organization of cooperation.

Web 2.0
Web 2.0 is a business term used to describe a generation of web applications built to foster user participation.

Whole Earth Catalog
The *Whole Earth Catalog* was a US paper-based magazine and product catalog with a focus on DIY.

Whole Earth 'Lectronic Link (WELL)
Whole Earth 'Lectronic Link (WELL) is one of the oldest operating virtual communities, founded in 1985, and follows the naming of the *Whole Earth Catalog*.

Wiki
Wiki is a web-based content management software that comes in the form of a system of interlinked hypertext documents.

Wikipedia
Wikipedia uses wiki software to enable volunteers to write articles on encyclopedic topics. It exists in more than three hundred language editions, and is the largest and highest-quality reference work ever created in many of them.

NOTES

Chapter 1

1. Yochai Benkler, *The Wealth of Networks: How Social Production Transforms Markets and Freedom* (Yale University Press, 2006).
2. Eric Klinenberg, *Palaces for the People: How Social Infrastructure Can Help Fight Inequality, Polarization, and the Decline of Civic Life* (Crown, 2018).
3. Charles M. Schweik and Robert C. English, *Internet Success: A Study of Open Source Software Commons* (MIT Press, 2012).
4. Elinor Ostrom, *Governing the Commons: The Evolution of Institutions for Collective Action* (Cambridge University Press, 1990).

Chapter 2

1. Richard M. Stallman, *Free Software, Free Society: Selected Essays of Richard M. Stallman*, ed. Joshua Gay (Free Software Foundation, 2002).
2. Richard Sennett, *Together: The Rituals, Pleasures and Politics of Co-Operation* (Penguin, 2013).
3. Michael Tomasello, Carol Dweck, Joan Silk, Brian Skyrms, and Elizabeth Spelke, *Why We Cooperate* (MIT Press, 2009).
4. Robert Darnton, *Business of Enlightenment: A Publishing History of the Encyclopédie, 1775–1800* (Harvard University Press, 1979).
5. Philipp Blom, *Enlightening the World: Encyclopédie, the Book That Changed the Course of History* (St. Martin's Press, 2005).
6. Sarah Ogilvie, *The Dictionary People: The Unsung Heroes Who Created the Oxford English Dictionary* (Alfred A. Knopf, 2023).
7. Robert C. Allen, "Collective Invention," *Journal of Economic Behavior & Organization* 4, no. 1 (March 1, 1983): 1–24, https://doi.org/10.1016/0167-2681(83)90023-9.
8. Elinor Ostrom, *Governing the Commons: The Evolution of Institutions for Collective Action* (Cambridge University Press, 1991).
9. Vincent Ostrom and Elinor Ostrom, "Public Goods and Public Choices," in *Alternatives for Delivering Public Services: Toward Improved Performance*, ed. Emanuel S. Savas (Westview Press, 1977), 7–49.
10. Garrett Hardin, "The Tragedy of the Commons," *Science* 162, no. 3859 (December 13, 1968): 1243–1248, https://doi.org/10.1126/science.162.3859

.1243. In addition to his dubious yet influential claims about the commons, Hardin espoused eugenicist, racist, and ethnonationalist beliefs.
11. Ronald H. Coase, "The Nature of the Firm," *Economica* 4, no. 16 (1937): 386–405, https://doi.org/10.1111/j.1468-0335.1937.tb00002.x.
12. Charlotte Hess and Elinor Ostrom, eds., *Understanding Knowledge as a Commons: From Theory to Practice* (MIT Press, 2011).
13. James Boyle, "The Second Enclosure Movement and the Construction of the Public Domain," *Law and Contemporary Problems* 66, no. 1 (April 1, 2003): 33–74.
14. Lawrence Lessig, *Code and Other Laws of Cyberspace* (Basic Books, 1999).
15. Stewart Brand, "Spacewar: Fanatic Life and Symbolic Death Among the Computer Bums," *Rolling Stone* 7 (1972): 50–58.
16. Janet Abbate, *Inventing the Internet* (MIT Press, 1999).
17. Fred Turner, *From Counterculture to Cyberculture: Stewart Brand, the Whole Earth Network, and the Rise of Digital Utopianism* (University of Chicago Press, 2008).
18. Kevin Driscoll, *The Modem World: A Prehistory of Social Media* (Yale University Press, 2022).
19. Fred Turner, "How Digital Technology Found Utopian Ideology: Lessons from the First Hackers' Conference," in *Critical Cyberculture Studies: Current Terrain, Future Directions*, ed. David Silver and Adrienne Massanari (NYU Press, 2006), 255–269.
20. Steven Levy, *Hackers: Heroes of the Computer Revolution* (Anchor Press, 1984).
21. Sam Williams, *Free as in Freedom: Richard Stallman's Crusade for Free Software* (O'Reilly Media, 2009).
22. Linus Torvalds and David Diamond, *Just for Fun: The Story of an Accidental Revolutionary* (Harper Business, 2002).
23. Eric S. Raymond, *The Cathedral and the Bazaar: Musings on Linux and Open Source by an Accidental Revolutionary*, ed. Tim O'Reilly (O'Reilly and Associates, 1999).
24. Yochai Benkler, "Coase's Penguin, or, Linux and the Nature of the Firm," *Yale Law Journal* 112, no. 3 (2002): 369–446, https://doi.org/10.2307/1562247.
25. Yochai Benkler, *The Wealth of Networks: How Social Production Transforms Markets and Freedom* (Yale University Press, 2006).

Chapter 3

1. "Android Statistics (2026)," Business of Apps, accessed January 26, 2026, https://www.businessofapps.com/data/android-statistics/.

2. Jim Giles, "Internet Encyclopaedias Go Head to Head," *Nature* 438, no. 7070 (December 14, 2005): 900–901, https://doi.org/10.1038/438900a.
3. John Herrman, "YouTube May Add to the Burdens of Humble Wikipedia," *New York Times*, March 19, 2018, https://www.nytimes.com/2018/03/19/business/media/youtube-wikipedia.html.
4. Brian Keegan, Darren Gergle, and Noshir Contractor, "Staying in the Loop: Structure and Dynamics of Wikipedia's Breaking News Collaborations," in *Proceedings of the Eighth Annual International Symposium on Wikis and Open Collaboration* (ACM, 2012), 1:1–10, https://doi.org/10.1145/2462932.2462934.
5. "List of Wikipedias," Wikimedia Foundation, accessed October 30, 2025, https://meta.wikimedia.org/w/index.php?title=List_of_Wikipedias&oldid=29438744.
6. "Fandom.com," Semrush, accessed May 22, 2024, https://www.semrush.com/website/fandom.com/overview/.
7. Connor McMahon, Isaac Johnson, and Brent Hecht, "The Substantial Interdependence of Wikipedia and Google: A Case Study on the Relationship Between Peer Production Communities and Information Technologies," in *Proceedings of the International AAAI Conference on Web and Social Media* 11, no. 1 (2017): 142–151, https://doi.org/10.1609/icwsm.v11i1.14883.
8. Neil Thompson and Douglas Hanley, "Science Is Shaped by Wikipedia: Evidence from a Randomized Control Trial," MIT Sloan Research Paper, February 13, 2018, https://papers.ssrn.com/abstract=3039505.
9. Marit Hinnosaar, Toomas Hinnosaar, Michael Kimmur, and Olga Slivko, "Wikipedia Matters," *Journal of Economics & Management Strategy* 32, no. 3 (2023): 657–669, https://doi.org/10.1111/jems.12421.
10. Yochai Benkler and Helen Nissenbaum, "Commons-Based Peer Production and Virtue," *Journal of Political Philosophy* 14, no. 4 (2006): 394–419, https://doi.org/10.1111/j.1467-9760.2006.00235.x.
11. Jérôme Hergueux, Emeric Henry, Yochai Benkler, and Yann Algan, "Social Exchange and the Reciprocity Roller Coaster: Evidence from the Life and Death of Virtual Teams," *Organization Science* 34, no. 6 (November 2023): 2296–2314, https://doi.org/10.1287/orsc.2021.1515; Yann Algan, Yochai Benkler, Mayo Fuster Morell, and Jérôme Hergueux, "Cooperation in a Peer Production Economy: Experimental Evidence from Wikipedia," SSRN Scholarly Paper (Rochester, NY, 2013), https://doi.org/10.2139/ssrn.2843518.
12. Shoshana Zuboff, *The Age of Surveillance Capitalism: The Fight for a Human Future at the New Frontier of Power* (Public Affairs, 2019).
13. "About Us," Open Directory Project, accessed on May 22, 2024, http://odp.org/about.html.

Chapter 4

1. Dana Lewis, "Do Something, Anything, for Someone Else, *DIYPS.org* (blog), January 23, 2026, https://diyps.org.
2. "Welcome to Nightscout," Nightscout Project, accessed May 23, 2024, http://www.nightscout.info/.
3. Rebecca Heilweil, "This Woman Designed—and Texts—Her Own Pancreas," *Forbes*, June 17, 2017, https://www.forbes.com/sites/rebeccaheilweil1/2017/06/15/this-woman-designed-and-texts-her-own-pancreas/?sh=3124185443b0.
4. Bo Leuf and Ward Cunningham, *The Wiki Way: Quick Collaboration on the Web* (Addison-Wesley Professional, 2001).
5. "Crowdsourcing Solutions to Empower Communities," Ushahidi, accessed May 23, 2024, https://www.ushahidi.com//.
6. Benjamin Mako Hill, "Essays on Volunteer Mobilization in Peer Production" (PhD diss., Massachusetts Institute of Technology, 2013), https://dspace.mit.edu/bitstream/handle/1721.1/86240/874134737-MIT.pdf.
7. Yochai Benkler, "Coase's Penguin, or, Linux and the Nature of the Firm," *Yale Law Journal* 112, no. 3 (2002): 369–446, https://doi.org/10.2307/1562247.
8. Jeremy Foote, Aaron Shaw, and Benjamin Mako Hill, "Communication Networks Do Not Predict Success in Attempts at Peer Production," *Journal of Computer-Mediated Communication* 28, no. 3 (May 1, 2023), https://doi.org/10.1093/jcmc/zmad002.
9. Aaron Shaw and Eszter Hargittai, "The Pipeline of Online Participation Inequalities: The Case of Wikipedia Editing," *Journal of Communication* 68, no. 1 (February 1, 2018): 143–168, https://doi.org/10.1093/joc/jqx003.
10. Edna Dias Canedo, Heloise Acco Tives, Madianita Bogo Marioti, Fabiano Fagundes, and José Antonio Siqueira de Cerqueira, "Barriers Faced by Women in Software Development Projects," *Information* 10, no. 10 (October 2019): 309, https://doi.org/10.3390/info10100309.
11. Christian Pentzold, "Grounding Peer Production in Practice: Editorial Routines and Everyday Engagement in the 'Free Encyclopedia Anyone Can Edit,'" *Communication, Culture and Critique* 11, no. 3 (September 1, 2018): 455–474, https://doi.org/10.1093/ccc/tcy010.

Chapter 5

1. Charles M. Schweik and Robert C. English, *Internet Success: A Study of Open source Software Commons* (MIT Press, 2012).
2. Nathan Schneider, "Admins, Mods, and Benevolent Dictators for Life: The Implicit Feudalism of Online Communities," *New Media & Society* 24, no. 9 (2022): 1965–1985, https://doi.org/10.1177/1461444820986553.

3. Marie Lebert, "Project Gutenberg (1971–2009)," 2009, https://www.gutenberg.org/files/31632/31632-pdf.pdf.
4. Aaron Halfaker, Aniket Kittur, and John Riedl, "Don't Bite the Newbies: How Reverts Affect the Quantity and Quality of Wikipedia Work," in *Proceedings of the 7th International Symposium on Wikis and Open Collaboration (WikiSym '11)* (ACM, 2011), 163–172, https://doi.org/10.1145/2038558.2038585.
5. "Croatian Wikipedia Disinformation Assessment–2021" (Wikimedia Foundation, 2021), https://meta.wikimedia.org/wiki/Croatian_Wikipedia_Disinformation_Assessment-2021.
6. Aniket Kittur and Robert E. Kraut, "Harnessing the Wisdom of Crowds in Wikipedia: Quality Through Coordination," in *Proceedings of the 2008 ACM Conference on Computer Supported Cooperative Work (CSCW '08)* (ACM, 2008), 37–46, https://doi.org/10.1145/1460563.1460572.
7. Dariusz Jemielniak, *Common Knowledge?: An Ethnography of Wikipedia* (Stanford University, 2014), 65–76.
8. Leah Buechley and Eric M. Eisenberg, "The LilyPad Arduino: Toward Wearable Engineering for Everyone," *IEEE Pervasive Computing* 7, no. 2 (2008): 12–15, https://doi.org/10.1109/MPRV.2008.38.
9. Leah Buechley and Benjamin Mako Hill, "LilyPad in the Wild: How Hardware's Long Tail Is Supporting New Engineering and Design Communities," in *Proceedings of the 8th ACM Conference on Designing Interactive Systems (DIS '10)* (ACM, 2010), 199–207, https://doi.org/10.1145/1858171.1858206.
10. Morgan G. Ames, *The Charisma Machine: The Life, Death, and Legacy of One Laptop per Child* (MIT Press, 2019).
11. Christina Dunbar-Hester, *Hacking Diversity: The Politics of Inclusion in Open Technology Cultures* (Princeton University Press, 2020).
12. Kaylea Champion and Benjamin Mako Hill, "Underproduction: An Approach for Measuring Risk in Open Source Software," in *2021 IEEE International Conference on Software Analysis, Evolution and Reengineering (SANER)* (IEEE, 2021), 388–399, https://doi.org/10.1109/SANER50967.2021.00043.
13. Jacob Thebault-Spieker, Brent Hecht, and Loren Terveen, "Geographic Biases Are 'Born, Not Made': Exploring Contributors' Spatiotemporal Behavior in OpenStreetMap," in *Proceedings of the 2018 ACM Conference on Supporting Groupwork (GROUP '18)* (ACM, 2018), 71–82, https://doi.org/10.1145/3148330.3148350.
14. Our use of the term diverges substantially from Piskorski, who focuses on marketing or sales failures that can be overcome with *more* social connection and interaction. As we discuss below, the social failures we present cannot necessarily be resolved through more social interaction alone but rather

require other mechanisms and interventions to correct biases as well as misalignments that emerge organically in social production. For the original, see Mikołaj Jan Piskorski, *A Social Strategy: How We Profit from Social Media* (Princeton University Press, 2014).

Chapter 6

1. Excerpts quoted in this chapter have been adapted from a text originally published online: Benjamin Mako Hill and Aaron Shaw, "Wikipedia and the End of Open Collaboration?," MIT Press, September 19, 2019, https://wikipedia20.mitpress.mit.edu/pub/lifecycles/release/2.
2. Nathan TeBlunthuis, Aaron Shaw, and Benjamin Mako Hill, "Revisiting 'The Rise and Decline' in a Population of Peer Production Projects," in *Proceedings of the 2018 CHI Conference on Human Factors in Computing Systems* (ACM, 2018), 355:1–355:7, https://doi.org/10.1145/3173574.3173929.
3. Yochai Benkler, "Coase's Penguin, or, Linux and the Nature of the Firm," *Yale Law Journal* 112, no. 3 (2002): 369–446, https://doi.org/10.2307/1562247.
4. Aaron Halfaker, R. Stuart Geiger, Jonathan T. Morgan, and John Riedl, "The Rise and Decline of an Open Collaboration System: How Wikipedia's Reaction to Popularity Is Causing Its Decline," *American Behavioral Scientist* 57, no. 5 (May 1, 2013): 664–688, https://doi.org/10.1177/0002764212469365; TeBlunthuis, Shaw, and Hill, "Revisiting 'The Rise and Decline' in a Population of Peer Production Projects."
5. John Seigenthaler, "A False Wikipedia 'Biography,'" *USA Today*, November 30, 2005, https://usatoday30.usatoday.com/news/opinion/editorials/2005-11-29-wikipedia-edit_x.htm; Katherine Q. Seelye, "Snared in the Web of a Wikipedia Liar," *New York Times*, December 4, 2005, sec. 4.
6. Sarah Mervosh, "North Face Edited Wikipedia's Photos. Wikipedia Wasn't Happy," *New York Times*, May 30, 2019, sec. Business, https://www.nytimes.com/2019/05/30/business/north-face-wikipedia-leo-burnett.html.
7. Rebecca Lefort and Ben Leapman, "MPs Accused of Wikipedia Expenses 'Cover-Up,'" *Telegraph*, May 8, 2010, sec. News, https://www.telegraph.co.uk/news/newstopics/mps-expenses/7696484/MPs-accused-of-Wikipedia-expenses-cover-up.html.
8. Fairbnb.coop, accessed May 23, 2024, https://fairbnb.coop/.
9. Stocksy United, accessed May 23, 2024, https://www.stocksy.com/.
10. Ethan Mollick, "Filthy Lucre? Innovative Communities, Identity, and Commercialization," *Organization Science* 27, no. 6 (December 1, 2016): 1472–1487, https://doi.org/10.1287/orsc.2016.1100.

11. Gordon Burtch, Dokyun Lee, and Zhichen Chen, "Generative AI Degrades Online Communities," *Communications of the ACM* 67, no. 3 (February 22, 2024): 40–42, https://doi.org/10.1145/3624732; Maria del Rio-Chanona, Nadzeya Laurentsyeva, and Johannes Wachs, "Are Large Language Models a Threat to Digital Public Goods? Evidence from Activity on Stack Overflow," arXiv, July 14, 2023, https://doi.org/10.48550/arXiv.2307.07367.

12. Tim Wu, *The Master Switch: The Rise and Fall of Information Empires* (Knopf Doubleday, 2011).

13. Abhishek Nagaraj and Henning Piezunka, "Motivating the Established, Deterring the New: The Divergent Effect of Platform Competition on Member Contributions in Digital Mapping Communities," *Academy of Management Global Proceedings* (April 2018): 81, https://journals.aom.org/doi/10.5465/amgblproc.surrey.2018.0081.abs.

FURTHER READING

The most influential treatise on peer production is Yochai Benkler's *The Wealth of Networks* (Yale University Press, 2006). An overview of conceptions and applications of peer production can be found in the *Handbook of Peer Production*, edited by Mathieu O'Neil, Sophie Toupin, and Christian Pentzold (Wiley, 2021). There are also several academic books published about FLOSS. These include Charles M. Schweik and Robert E. English's *Internet Success: A Study of Open source Software Commons* (MIT Press, 2012), which provides empirical analyses, Johan Söderberg's theoretically driven *Hacking Capitalism: The Free and Open Software Movement* (Routledge, 2012) as well as anthropological accounts in E. Gabriella Coleman's *Coding Freedom: The Ethics and Aesthetics of Hacking* (Princeton University Press, 2012) and Christopher M. Kelty's *Two Bits: The Cultural Significance of Free Software* (Duke University Press, 2008).

Two books on FLOSS aimed at more general audiences are Eric S. Raymond's *Cathedral and the Bazaar: Musings on Linux and Open Source by an Accidental Revolutionary* (O'Reilly, 2009), a collection of essays by the person who coined the term "open source," and Karl Fogel's *Producing Open Source Software* (O'Reilly, 2009), a how-to manual for running an open source software project.

A broad perspective on user-generated content and online collaboration is offered by Robert E. Kraut and Paul Resnick's *Building Successful Online Communities* (MIT Press, 2011) as well as Mathieu O'Neil's *Cyberchiefs* (Pluto Press, 2008) and Axel Bruns's *Blogs, Wikipedia, Second Life, and Beyond: From Production to Produsage* (Peter Lang, 2008).

A series of popular and journalistic accounts of online collaboration have also described peer production as a part of a larger conversation. These include Clay Shirky's *Here Comes Everybody* (Penguin, 2008), Cass Sunstein's *Infotopia* (Oxford University Press, 2006), and Yochai Benkler's *The Penguin and the Leviathan* (Crown Currency, 2011).

INDEX

BENJAMIN MAKO HILL is a social scientist and technologist. In both roles, he works to understand the social dynamics that shape online communities. His work focuses on communities engaged in the peer production of digital public goods—like Wikipedia and Linux. He is an associate professor in the Department of Communication at the University of Washington and a founding member of the Community Data Science Collective. Hill is also a faculty associate at the Berkman Klein Center for Internet & Society at Harvard University. In addition, he has been an activist, developer, contributor, and leader in the FLOSS and free culture movements for more than two decades as part of the Debian, Ubuntu, and Wikimedia projects.

CHRISTIAN PENTZOLD is a professor and the chair of media and communications in the Department of Communication and Media Studies at Leipzig University. Before that, he worked in the Center for Media, Communication and Information Research at the University of Bremen as well as at Chemnitz University of Technology. In Leipzig, Pentzold is one of the codirectors of the Center for Digital Participation. He is broadly interested in people's everyday use of digital media along with the roles that information and communication technologies play in modern societies. His work in communication research and media analysis links to insights coming from cultural sociology, linguistics, and science and technology studies. In current projects, he studies automation in the public sector, digital political participation, big data and public sense making, citizen-driven innovation in journalism, and the experience of time in algorithmic media. Beyond that, Pentzold is interested in cocreation and arts-based methods as well as in applying theories of practice to the study of media and communication.

AARON SHAW is a professor of communication studies and sociology (by courtesy) at Northwestern University, where he is affiliated with the Center for Human-Computer Interaction + Design, Institute for Policy Research, and Buffett Institute for Global Affairs. Shaw is also a faculty associate of the Berkman Klein Center for Internet & Society at Harvard University, cofounder of the Community Data Science Collective, and a former fellow at the Center for Advanced Study in the Behavioral Sciences at Stanford University. Most of his research investigates organizing, participation, and governance in online communities that create peer produced public information goods like Wikipedia or the Linux operating system.

Publisher contact:
The MIT Press
Massachusetts Institute of Technology
77 Massachusetts Avenue, Cambridge, MA 02139
mitpress.mit.edu

EU Authorised Representative:
Easy Access System Europe, Mustamäe tee 50,
10621 Tallinn, Estonia
gpsr.requests@easproject.com

Printed by Integrated Books International,
United States of America